Thriving Systems Theory and Metaphor-Driven Modeling

T0137248

Leslie J. Waguespack

Thriving Systems Theory and Metaphor-Driven Modeling

 Springer

Leslie J. Waguespack
Bentley University
Waltham, MA
USA
lwaguespack@bentley.edu

ISBN 978-1-4471-6214-8   ISBN 978-1-84996-302-2 (eBook)
DOI 10.1007/978-1-84996-302-2
Springer London Dordrecht Heidelberg New York

British Library Cataloguing in Publication Data
A catalogue record for this book is available from the British Library

Printed on acid-free paper

Springer is part of Springer Science+Business Media (www.springer.com)

Acknowledgments

If the quest for understanding systems quality in this monograph has been challenging, the task of acknowledging all the contributions that have brought me to these ideas is impossible. At the core of this journey was a simple question, "How can you tell whether one model of a system is better than another?" The question emanates from my teaching of modeling in the object-oriented paradigm over the past two decades. I usually begin my lectures on this topic by declaring, "There are no perfect models but there are useful ones and some models are better than others." After dozens of courses teaching OO modeling to undergraduate students, graduate students and practicing software professionals and repeating this declaration countless times, I began the quest to justify the statement with some rational validation greater than my intuition and 45 years of teaching and software development experience. This monograph is my validation effort.

My first acknowledgement must go to Christopher Alexander whose writings on physical architecture provide not only the substance on which I have assembled my *Thriving Systems Theory*, but also on the mode of rational investigation and argument that he models in his four volume treatise on *The Nature of Order*. That work is both illuminating and inspiring in its approach to expressing knowledge and understanding.

I must recognize all those students who were brave enough to allow me to "bend" their minds with an object-oriented view of the world and describing the things in it. My colleagues at Bentley University granted me sabbatical with the dedicated time to wander and explore the questions of models and systems which led me to Alexander, Lakoff and Brooks. Two of those Bentley colleagues in the Computer Information Systems department generously engaged in countless hours of discussion (and argument) with me over both the content and the mode of expressing the ideas in this monograph: Bill Schiano and David Yates, fast colleagues and dear friends. It is with their continued collaboration I hope to bring these ideas beyond theory into practice. Special thanks to Jennifer Xu for her guidance in the cluster analysis. Two other notable influences are colleagues at the University of South Alabama who arranged for a colloquium visit where I was able to share my questions and test my ambitions for this monograph project: Roy Daigle and Bart Longenecker.

As Lakoff would put it, the layers of metaphors through which I understand systems and software were built up over a lifetime of learning: primary parochial education with the Sisters of the Sacred Heart and a secondary education with the Christian Brothers of Saint John Baptist de La Salle. At the University of Louisiana at Lafayette (formerly the University of Southwestern Louisiana), I earned computer science degrees, a B.S., an M.S. directed by Dr. James R. Oliver and a doctorate under the direction of Professors Bruce Shriver, Wayne Anderson, and Ted Lewis. Endless hours of study and exploration of programming languages, computer architecture, and virtual machine architecture and theory were had with fellow graduate students: Steve Landry, Sam Bullard, Denny Hyams, and Doug Robertson. My years at the United State Air Force Manpower and Personnel Center introduced me to the practical realities and challenges of managing very large databases and trans-global transaction systems. My project management and systems architecture ideas evolved working with Ted Hann, Don Moore, Gary Filipski, and John Newton.

My family deserves the majority of my thanks for their patience and support during formation of this work: my loving and devoted spouse, Blanche, and my children: Michael, Patricia, Peter, and Paul, all of whom have plied careers in the computing industry and inspire me with their energy and resilience.

Finally, I offer my deepest thanks to my father, Leslie (Sr.), and my mother, Catherine. They are always my first and best teachers in the values of life and living and the font of all the goodness and faith that has showered my life.

Contents

Chapter 1
Introduction

The centrality of computer-based information systems at this juncture in the evolution of human society and commerce cannot be overemphasized. There is virtually no aspect of human living that is not affected at least indirectly by the role and function of information systems, particularly in business. They influence the quality of life. The effectiveness and efficiency of any system (e.g. business information system) relies heavily on the fidelity that the system achieves in matching function to context not only at its inception, but throughout the life of the human system it supports. The evolution of an information system in concert with the surrounding social activities is a key factor in its cost-effectiveness and competitive advantage in the commercial domain.

The earliest definitions of computer-based information system success revolved around reducing computer downtime and eliminating the "mistakes" in software that limited system availability. The development life cycle of many systems was measured in half-decades. Today, information system stakeholders expect development life cycles measured in months and adaptation or realignment of computer-based functionality in a few weeks, if not days. Achievements like these require an extreme level of coordination and integration in the modeling used to assimilate, analyze, and represent the various aspects of the information system throughout its life span.

What characteristics would models need to achieve these efficiencies? How would these models be judged to meet the criteria of stakeholder satisfaction? What would constitute a good model, a great model? And what processes would need to be in place to achieve good, even great models? For at least the last 50 years, software engineering has wrestled with these questions. What is different in this writing is the casting of these questions from a different perspective – an attempt to unify the treatment of system knowledge within a single, unifying theory of modeling quality. This monograph explores the qualities that define good, even great, system models for whatever purpose: requirements, analysis, design, implementation, business, or business process.

L.J. Waguespack, *Thriving Systems Theory and Metaphor-Driven Modeling*,
DOI 10.1007/978-1-84996-302-2_1, © Springer-Verlag London Limited 2010

1.1   The Quest for Great Design: Great Designers

The formation and education of system professionals who are adept at developing effective and efficient information systems has been a major quest of computer science, management information systems, and systems engineering for at least the last half-century. The role of designer in systems development has been characterized as artist, craftsman, scientist, and engineer. The development tools and methods of these IS disciplines are myriad and (for the most part) are well understood in their application. However, these disciplines do not consistently develop designers who produce predictably excellent results. The recipe for good choices in time, place, tool, and task are not understood so well. Preparing excellent designers and building effective and efficient information systems remain a challenge.

Fred Brooks in 1987 framed the challenge in "No Silver Bullet: Essence and Accidents of Software Engineering." In the face of all the advances in software engineering to that time, Brooks noted that the performance of systems designers was not always reliable or even well understood.

> Whereas the difference between poor conceptual designs and good ones may lie in the soundness of design-method, the difference between good designs and great ones surely does not. Great designs come from great designers. Software construction is a creative process. Sound methodology can empower and liberate the creative mind; it cannot inflame or inspire the drudge.
> The differences are not minor – they are rather like the differences between Salieri and Mozart. Study after study shows that the very best designers produce structures that are faster, smaller, simpler, cleaner and produced with less effort. [...] The differences between the great and the average approach an order of magnitude. [1]

Perhaps, any lack of satisfaction with the overall success of system design or system designers lies in a lack of clarity as to what constitutes "success." And thus, perhaps what designers lack in their preparation is a reference for assessing their design choices not in their distinct, minute detail, but in their integration in the composition of the system as a whole. In search of clarity, our exploration turns outside the aforementioned disciplines to gain a new perspective on building and understanding things as they fit into the "real world."

1.2   Building Buildings and Systems

The quest for synergy between building systems and the life that goes on in and around them motivates the work of Christopher Alexander, architect and philosopher. His early seminal works on architectural principles (pattern languages, in particular) have influenced not only buildings and civic planning but also the construction of software and systems. The reflection on systems in this monograph draws extensively from his more recent writings explaining the underlying organizational principles that address fundamental concepts of natural order leading to his pattern language of building. Alexander describes the goal of building as achieving *life*[1] through a structure-preserving process of transformation. This process and its underlying principles are here applied to modeling and constructing information systems. It is Alexander's characterization of *life* that herein proposes the definition of successful information system development that we seek. And in concert with Fred Brooks' reflection on design above, we seek not only to produce systems with the *life* that may be possible through sound methodology, but systems that *thrive* as they resonate and nurture the ecology of their environment and their stakeholders.

1.3 Humans Know and How They Know It

In conceiving and perceiving information systems as living structures, the greatest challenge is to identify the essence of purpose to preserve and extend as a system evolves in concert with its context. This requires a conceptual tool to form, represent, explain, and communicate system understanding that preserves the essence and enables the transforming evolution – the ongoing *life* of the system. For this purpose, I turn to the work of George Lakoff and colleagues as our guide with research-based theories in linguistics and cognitive psychology that present an intriguing explanation of the process of human thought and reasoning. I fuse their work based on the role of metaphor in knowledge and understanding with Alexander's ideas on quality building to explore the crafting of quality abstractions, models. And in so doing, I explore the limits of effectively communicating design concepts among stakeholders and developers to expose and clarify the details against which development success and system quality should be measured.

1.4 A Fusion of Perception, Conception, and Construction

Alexander's vision of *living structure* together with Lakoff's explanation of knowledge and understanding via metaphorical mechanisms provides an innovative framework for advancing the design and construction of effective and efficient information systems. I use the framework to examine system and software engineering principles and practices both for the purpose of studying them and exploiting their potential in information system development. The remainder of this monograph is divided into two parts.

---

[1] Several terms in this writing are adopted with specialized meanings that are quite distinct from their nominal meanings found in everyday language. Some of these terms derive from writings referencing other authors. Others are adopted here to reflect specific meanings in the context of this monograph. Terms with specialized meanings are denoted in italics such as *life* with the intention of reminding the reader of that specialized meaning.

Part one is composed of Chapters 2–6 and introduces *Thriving Systems Theory*. Thriving Systems Theory is a design quality framework with its roots in Christopher Alexander's insights into physical architecture and his *living structure* theory in architectural design.

Chapter 2 explores Christopher Alexander's conception of the order in natural things introducing a framework for understanding art, physical buildings, and their architecture. He introduces the concept of *wholeness* forming a basis for assessing the quality of a system. In examining *wholeness*, Alexander identifies *centers* as the building blocks of architectural form and identifies 15 properties of *center* intensity that in composition result in a system's *wholeness*.

To understand information systems in Alexander's terms, Chapter 3 maps his 15 properties of *centers* onto *choice* properties, characteristics commonly associated with design principles of information systems. The chapter concludes with a summary of those properties and their interrelationships.

Chapter 4 revisits the 15 *choice* properties derived from Alexander's *center* properties. This discussion extends the understanding of *choice* properties as discernible elements of the existing models by exploring the actions employed by modelers and designers to transform modeling elements and thus strengthen their *choice* properties. Coupled to modeling actions, the *choice* properties are not only observable characteristics but achievable design elements.

Chapter 5 examines Alexander's theory of *life* and the *generative building process* as it may be applied to building information systems. This chapter explores the life cycle of information systems and the correspondence to architecture including complexity and implementation choices. The chapter concludes by considering the designer's mindset required for building *living structure*.

Chapter 6 explores the field-effect of the 15 *choice* properties in achieving a *thriving information system*. Alexander's own analysis of the interproperty support relationships leads to a parallel matrix of supporting *choice* properties. Cluster analysis reveals an overarching definition of system qualities to describe systems that not only achieve survival of the *life* that reflects the system's purpose, but also exhibit a capacity for growth embracing the evolving, the *unfolding* requirements of the stakeholder community.

Part two is composed of Chapters 7–14 and explores a metamorphosis of systems development and management through the unifying infusion of Thriving Systems Theory. Through the strategy of *Metaphor-Driven Modeling*, the properties and qualities of *Thriving Systems Theory* are superimposed to guide requirements, analysis, design, and engineering.

Chapter 7 introduces the cognitive and linguistic theory of metaphorology as formulated by George Lakoff and colleagues. This discussion explains the theory of categorization, recognition, and understanding that underpin Lakoff's explanation of learning and cognitive processing. Applied to information systems, the metaphor is a stakeholder-friendly conceptual framework for capturing, transmitting, and processing system design information from one model instantiation to another. The metaphor's descriptive and expressive features fuse effectively with Alexander's conception of *centers*. Lakoff's theories both form a basis for explaining Alexander's notion of the human perception of order as well as provide a foundation for guiding the design and modeling *choices* to produce *living structure*.

Chapter 8 applies Lakoff's structure of conceptual metaphor to system characteristics and model features and incorporates Fred Brooks' explanation of *essence* and *accidents*. The ability to discriminate between essential stakeholder intentions and accidental choices of opportunity relates directly to effectively achieving *wholeness*. Given the myriad of distractions that can influence the crafting of system models, Fred Brooks reminds the modeler that his/her focus must remain fixed on discerning what is essential and what is not. In so doing, it is possible to maximize the property strength of modeling *choices* as they are addressed appropriately as either *essence* or *accident*.

Chapter 9 explores the role of methodology and life cycle in preserving system *life*. Virtually, every system life cycle involves several models either representing different paradigms and/or as a series of iterations. The multiplicity of models depicting the same system presents challenges in the *life*-preserving process. The transition from one model to the next involves various transforms that affect the content and *life* of the system. Each transform increases or decreases the intensity of *life* in the model. Alexander describes the evolution of a model as *unfolding* and this chapter explores his interpretation as applied to the system life cycle.

Chapter 10 examines the relationship of the sibling disciplines of software and systems engineering to *living* systems. There is a critical distinction to be explored between the modeling task from a system perspective versus the same from a software perspective. In each, the term architecture often connotes a static, almost permanent structure. Architecture in living systems is better described as a template that shapes a continuously evolving organism. This evolution, *unfolding*, is presented in the framework of metaphor-driven modeling. This template enables and frames the opportunity for efficiency and effectiveness.

Chapter 11 explores the question "What is system quality?" Is quality objective? Is quality subjective? Does subjective quality pertain only to art? What does it mean to say that "This or that is beautiful?" The chapter presents a four-part model of observer experience: mindset, expectation, threshold, and implementation. These parts are juxtaposed with Alexander's concepts of *wholeness*, Lakoff's explanation of understanding and cognition, and Brooks' categorization of *essence* and *accidents*. Finally, this framework of beauty and the *Thriving Systems Theory* are compared.

Chapter 12 provides a pragmatic context within which the reader can consider the properties of modeling developed in earlier chapters as they may be applied in practice – within the object-oriented paradigm. The principles and practices of a structure preserving process are essentially orthogonal to any particular design or programming paradigm in the sense that all modeling paradigms are about representation and transformation. However, to bring the strengthening process of *choice* properties into sharper focus and demonstrate the practical application of these theories in systems development, this chapter explores the application of these properties by way of object-oriented systems engineering.

Chapter 13 follows the lead of Chapter 12 by illustrating the potential for applying the principles and practices of a structure-preserving process by way of the relational paradigm. The relational paradigm is chosen because of its breadth of adoption in information systems development and because of its contrast to the object-oriented paradigm. That contrast demonstrates the challenge that any paradigm presents in the pursuit of modeling quality while at the same time exposing the orthogonal nature of the *choice* properties relative to any particular modeling paradigm.

Chapter 14 concludes the journey through thriving systems, models as metaphors, and the *life*-preserving transformational process of systems development. It reprises the major arguments for conceiving and representing systems as living metaphors. It invites the reader to consider applying the concept of *wholeness* and *Thriving Systems Theory* to a broader context of modeling beyond information systems to that of business models and business process models as well – positing that the 15 *choice* properties are equally evident in any system be it "natural" or "engineered!"

1.5   A Note of Disclosure to the Reader

In respect to you, the reader, it is appropriate to comment on the mode of persuasion attempted in this exposition. The practiced reader in the disciplines of computer science or information science will recognize an absence of mathematical formulae and algorithmic constructions. The practiced reader of management information systems or organizational behavior will recognize the absence of surveys, statistically tested null hypotheses, and the interpretations thereof. The absence of these implements of persuasion so comfortable to practitioners in these fields should hint that this writing is an academic discussion somewhat out of the ordinary.

The ideas and propositions that follow are not at the stage of provability but rather are postulation. The primary arguments associate and relate concepts that proceed from three very distinct intellectual perspectives. In this, the goal is to encourage builders of information systems to consider a new, innovative perspective with which to assess the value, the quality, of the constructions they envision and implement. I align well-respected findings and theories projecting the significance of one concept on another by exposing what I believe are largely intuitive, self-evident correlations once the concepts are explained in the manner chosen here. The explanations draw predominantly from a practitioner's perspective encouraging the reader to be an active participant by recalling personal experience reframed by the perspectives offered here.

What follows are steps on a path of investigation and discovery rather than the final results of a journey completed. Join in the journey with me.

Reference

1. Brooks FP, "No Silver Bullet: Essence and Accidents of Software Engineering," Computer, Vol. 20, No. 4 (April 1987) pp 10–19.

Part I
Thriving Systems Theory

The first part of the journey is determining your goal.

Chapter 2
Christopher Alexander's Nature of Order

Christopher Alexander is an oft-referenced icon for the concept of patterns in programming languages and design [1–3]. Alexander himself set forth his theory of good architectural design and its pursuit via architectural patterns in three books published in the latter half of the 1970s [4–6]. In a follow-up to his three-volume architectural exposition, he published a four-volume treatise on The Nature of Order that extensively examines his underlying theory and philosophy of *wholeness* and the properties of *life* in systems [7–10].[1]

This chapter examines Alexander's theory with the goal of correlating the principles and concepts of his treatise on *living structure* with the practice of modeling, analysis, and design of information systems. Although his central focus as an architect is on physical design as in building and construction, his theory goes to the heart of the process of creating systems that are effective and efficient.

Alexander's four book series, The Nature of Order, follows some 20 years after his earlier works on architectural patterns, A Pattern Language and The Timeless Way of Building. These two books are almost always cited as the genesis for the concept of patterns found in object-oriented systems engineering – most notably in Gamma [2] and Coplien [1]. In The Nature of Order, Alexander decomposes the conclusions and directives of those earlier works in a methodical explanation of their genesis in the principles of what he names the *living structure*. He accomplishes this by extensive excursions into contemporary theory and research reported in chemistry, physics, astronomy, biology, art, and engineering. Alexander's use of the term *life* is manifold drawing on its characteristics of evolution and growth, on its characteristics of nurture and interdependency, and on its fragility. In Book I and Book II, Alexander identifies "pattern" as a fundamentally informative characteristic of *life*. He draws out this theme as both a means of defining the existence of *life* in a structure and as a means (in patterned creations) of forming what he calls *living structures*. As he explains, "living structures are the result of a structure preserving process of becoming" [8, p. 4]. As these assertions are explored and explained,

---

[1]References noted as Book I, Book II, Book III, or Book IV refer to the four books in the series on *The Nature of Order.*

L.J. Waguespack, *Thriving Systems Theory and Metaphor-Driven Modeling,*
DOI 10.1007/978-1-84996-302-2_2, © Springer-Verlag London Limited 2010

Alexander defines *life* as it is manifest in physical architecture, its measurable characteristics, and the stepwise transformations that make up any process that is capable of producing a *living structure*.

The discussion that follows maps Alexander's theory and philosophy of building and architecture onto modeling and developing information systems and their architecture. It would be convenient to say that his thinking can be directly applied without any "interpretation"; however, his writings are rather clearly fixed on the physical architecture of rooms, buildings, towns, and cities. Although he cites work in information systems that have drawn on his vision of architecture, he is clearly preoccupied with a strong disaffection of what he calls a "mass psychosis, a half century of lifeless architectural design and construction" [7, p. 6]. His intention seems clearly focused on rehabilitating the practice of architecture in physical construction. Nonetheless, I shall show that the principles that Alexander develops to study *life* in buildings are entirely applicable to the modeling, design, and implementation of information systems.

2.1 Order, Complexity, and Human Perception

In Alexander's discussion of order, he settles on an understanding, based primarily on process, that the arrangement of things is based on their arrival at relative positions influenced by forces that guide their movement or evolution [7, p. 8]. The forces result from the relative location or context in which an element resides. Continuously influenced by these forces order emerges and is preserved over time, across space, or through change as elements systematically conform as constituent components of a whole. Arrangements that fail to achieve *wholeness* falling outside the equilibrium of these forces will not have sufficient stability to persist. In time, they must and will realign and in the meantime appear to exhibit disorder. In the millennia of human existence and evolution, the *wholeness* evidenced by the persistent arrangements has informed what humans have come to understand as "natural." In the world around us, we understand this as a result of the "laws of nature" and hence we perceive the world around us to be almost universally "natural" (with the probable exception of many human constructions).

A key concept in Alexander's theory is that order is a dynamic concept rather than a static one. Although humans often experience a large number of components or relationships as complexity, multiplicity does not automatically result in disorder. Neither does order naturally result from a small number of parts or relationships. It is not multiplicity that results in disorder but rather, an inability to comprehend an evolutionary, organizing, and explicative path of change from one arrangement to another and so forth and so on. As a result, human attempts to create and sustain orderly systems must rely on devising or (in Alexander's case) discovering rules for system construction that preserve the clearly visible, orderly composition and *unfolding* transformation of system and parts. Systems (natural or human-made) that entail this concept of order are said to have *life* [7, p. 33]. And thus, Alexander argues that methods of constructing living systems will always be based on techniques that preserve the natural order of *living structure*.

Alexander's research over 30 years with observers of architecture reports a remarkable fact that is corroborated by researchers in related fields. Given any two systems presented as visual images to the same population of observers, the vast majority of those observers (in excess of 80%) will agree on which of the two systems exhibits a greater degree of *life* [7, p. 71]. Alexander concludes that within a certain sphere of culture, there are almost universally held conceptions of order, which are evidenced by the feelings of *life* experienced by observers viewing images, structures, rooms, buildings, roads, or landscapes. He further asserts that this concept extends to any space in which objects and their relationships may be observed.

Can Alexander's theories be translated for constructing models of information systems that exhibit *life*? It would appear so! If (1) Alexander's "any space" extends beyond building physical artifacts to "building" conceptual artifacts and (2) the same principles of order govern models of systems constructed in a conceptual space, then (3) models of information systems possess the same relative degrees of *life* attributable in physical buildings and architecture. The task of confirming the assertion that models of information systems have *life* begins by considering the underlying principles of Alexander's concept of order.

2.2   Wholeness and Centers

Alexander's explanation of *life* in structures would seem to most readers to be more of a poetic rather than a scientific argument. Alexander's concept of *life* asserts that reality lies not on either end of a philosophical continuum with poetry and science at either end, but with a realization that poetry and science are simply different views of the same reality. *Life* arises from a system of constituents that contribute to a shared identity and purpose, a concept Alexander names *wholeness* where each part's structure and function flows into a continuity of the whole [7, p. 80]. Each of these contributing parts Alexander calls a *center*, "a distinct set of points in space, which, because of its organization, because of its internal coherence and because of its relation to its context, exhibits centeredness, forms a local zone of relative centeredness with respect to the other parts of space" [7, p. 84]. The term *center* reflects a need for focus to identify a coherent concept: first, how that concept contributes by itself to the whole of a system of parts, and second, how that concept works together in concert with the *centers* around it to contribute to the whole. In a phenomenon Alexander calls "field effect" each *center* impacts the whole in a way similar to a gravitational field sending out waves of influence to all the *centers* within its range of influence, interacting with neighbors and the collection that composes the whole [7, p. 119].

2.3   Choices as Centers

Alexander's conception of *wholeness* and *centers* is grounded in the geometry of space and its physical attributes of position and distance. To apply Alexander's concepts of physical structure to information systems, they must first be translated from a language of physical space to a language of cognitive space where physical position and distance correspond to concepts and consonance in "fields" populated by abstractions rather than shapes. The term *choice* serves well for that translation of Alexander's term *center* into this cognitive space.

An information system is an organized and integrated collection of *choices*. Some of those *choices* designate the stakeholders' understanding as to the purpose of the system. These are sometimes called requirements. Some of those *choices* designate the operations that explain the behavior of the system. These are sometimes called functional requirements. Some of those *choices* designate information that records the history of system activities and accumulates information as it goes forward. These are sometimes called data requirements. Some of those *choices* designate points where the activities that go on outside the system come in contact with the system and are called interfaces. Some of those *choices* designate representations that will characterize elements in the implementation of the system. These are sometimes called design decisions. Traditionally, these *choices* are taken at different times and reflect a conviction toward organizing activities that eventually result in a working information system. A collection of the kinds of these *choices* and a particular sequence of activities that produces them is sometimes called a development methodology. In modeling and information systems, these *choices* are exactly Alexander's *centers*. And in Alexander's terms, the degree to which these *choices* contribute to the whole (system) determines to what degree the system has *life*.

Choices are the *centers* that lie at the root of *life* in information systems. *Choices* address different aspects of system abstraction at different points or stages in system development. A *choice* by nature admits to alternatives and the prospect of reconsideration when an *unfolding* context of experience and understanding merits it. Alexander uses this term, *unfolding*, repeatedly to explain the evolution of an architectural conception toward a useful intensification of *life*. In this sense, a living information system model *unfolds* revealing a continuity of structure and function and consonance with the context within which it is intended to serve.

2.4   Wholeness and Center Properties

Wholeness (as Alexander describes it) is a "field" of interrelationships among *centers* in a "space" where the interaction of the *centers* resonates with the "self" of the "observer." Alexander defines *wholeness* as follows:

> I propose a view of physical reality which is dominated by the existence of this one particular structure, W, the wholeness. In any given region of space, some sub-regions have higher

intensity as **centers**; others have less. Many sub-regions have weak intensity or none at all. The overall configurations of the nested centers, together with their relative intensities, comprise a single structure. I define this structure as "the" wholeness of that region. [7, p. 96]

Wholeness is palpable. In a system comprising strong *centers*, the *wholeness* "feels strong." To say that a system has *"life"* is to say that the system's *wholeness* resonates with the observer. The fact that a majority of observers consistently share the same relative feeling of *life* (as in the image experiments with Alexander's students) results from the observers' shared culture, a communal understanding about what order is in their world. The "feeling of *life*," the *wholeness* of systems, derives from identifiable (and in some cases quantifiable) properties that define each and every *center* and its relationships in the whole.

Alexander identifies 15 properties of *centers* that contribute to the degree of *life* experienced by an observer. In Alexander's list, the properties are expressed in terms of architectural visualization although he says that these properties are equally applicable to "actions:"

> Quantum mechanics asserts, via the mathematics, that particles are physically affected in their behavior by the wholeness of the space in which they move.... [Wholeness] is not restricted to buildings or works of art, but is valid and essential even in those parts of the world we have historically believed to be mechanical in nature. [7, p. 467]

Table 2.1 lists the 15 properties in Alexander's architectural vision of centers with the description of each [7, pp. 239–241].

Table 2.1 Alexander's properties of *Centers*

Property	Description
1. Levels of scale	The way that a strong center is made stronger partly by smaller strong centers contained in it and partly by its larger strong centers that contain it.
2. Strong centers	Defines the way that a strong center requires a special field-like effect, created by other centers, as a primary source of its strength.
3. Boundaries	The way that the field-like effect of a center is strengthened by the creation of a ring-like center, made of smaller centers that surround and intensify the former. The boundary also unites the center with the centers beyond it, thus strengthening it further.
4. Alternating repetition	The way in which centers are strengthened when they repeat, by the insertion of other centers between the repeating ones.
5. Positive space	The way that a given center must draw its strength, in part, from the strength of other centers immediately adjacent to it in space.
6. Good shape	The way that the strength of a given center depends on its actual shape and the way this effect requires that even the shape, its boundary, and the space around it are made up of strong centers.
7. Local symmetries	The way that the intensity of a given center is increased by the extent to which other smaller centers that it contains are themselves arranged in locally symmetrical groups.
8. Deep interlock and ambiguity	The way in which the intensity of a given center can be increased when it is attached to nearby strong centers, through a third set of strong centers that ambiguously belong to both.

(continued)

Table 2.1   (continued)

Property	Description
9. Contrast	The way that a center is strengthened by the sharpness of the distinction between its character and the character of surrounding centers.
10. Gradients	The way in which a center is strengthened by a graded series of different-sized centers that then "point" to the new center and intensify its field effect.
11. Roughness	The way that the field effect of a given center draws its strength, necessarily, from irregularities in the sizes, shapes, and arrangements of other nearby centers.
12. Echoes	The way that the strength of a given center depends on similarities of angle and orientation and systems of centers forming characteristic angles, thus forming larger centers, among the centers it contains.
13. The void	The way that the intensity of every center depends on the existence of a still place – an empty center – somewhere in its field.
14. Simplicity and inner calm	The way the strength of a center depends on its simplicity – on the process of reducing the number of different centers that exist in it, while increasing the strength of these centers to make them weigh more.
15. Not separateness	The way the life and strength of a center depends on the extent to which that center is merged smoothly – sometimes even indistinguishably – with the centers that form its surroundings.

References

1. Coplien J and Schmidt D, Eds., *Pattern Languages of Program Design*, Reading, MA: Addison-Wesley, 1995.
2. Gamma E, Helm R, Johnson R and Vlissides J, *Design Patterns: Elements of Reusable Object-Oriented Software*, Reading, MA: Addison-Wesley, 1995.
3. Coad P, "Object-Oriented Patterns," *Communications of the ACM*, 35, 9 [September 1992]: 152–159.
4. Alexander C, *A Timeless Way of Building*, New York: Oxford University Press, 1979.
5. Alexander C, Ishikawa S, Silverstein M, Jacobson M, Fiksdahl-King I and Angel S, *A Pattern Language*, New York: Oxford University Press, 1977.
6. Alexander C, Silverstein M, Angel S, Ishikawa S and Abrams D, *The Oregon Experiment*, New York: Oxford University Press, 1975.
7. Alexander C, *The Nature of Order An Essay on the Art of Building and the Nature of the Universe: Book I - The Phenomenon of Life*, Berkeley, CA: The Center for Environmental Structure, 2002.
8. Alexander C, *The Nature of Order An Essay on the Art of Building and the Nature of the Universe: Book II - The Process of Creating Life*, Berkeley, CA: The Center for Environmental Structure, 2002.
9. Alexander C, *The Nature of Order An Essay on the Art of Building and the Nature of the Universe: Book III - A Vision of a Living World*, Berkeley, CA: The Center for Environmental Structure, 2005.
10. Alexander C, *The Nature of Order An Essay on the Art of Building and the Nature of the Universe: Book IV - The Luminous Ground*, Berkeley, CA: The Center for Environmental Structure, 2004.

Chapter 3
Wholeness and Center Properties Mapped to Modeling

Assessing the intensity of *life* in an information system requires a determination of what *wholeness* means in that context. This chapter presents a mapping of the 15 properties of *centers* onto modeling and information systems. Recall that Alexander's *centers* are translated as the concept of *choices* in the cognitive space of information systems, so it is with the 15 property descriptions that follow. Each property in the list below is first defined in Alexander's architectural terms and then expressed in terms of modeling *choices* [1]. To complete the translation, each *center* property is expressed as a term more closely aligned with modeling in information systems.

3.1 Levels of Scale to Stepwise Refinement

A way that a strong center is made stronger partly by smaller strong centers contained in it and partly by its larger strong centers which contain it.

Choices in information system modeling are often manifest through some arrangement of modularization. Modules regularly organize and enclose a concept representing a chosen characterization of knowledge or understanding about the system behavior being modeled. As the natural human process of problem-solving often engages "divide and conquer" as a means of converting a question into "bite-sized pieces," so modules define both the pieces and how they interrelate in both the decomposition and composition of a system. In this vein, Levels of Scale describes the effectiveness with which the "bite-size pieces" subdivide the problem into manageable parts. Are the parts naturally and recognizably distinct? Are the criteria and process of splitting apart into pieces self-evident and readily repeatable? Are the parts readily disposed to recombination? These last two questions reflect on the ability of the partitioning criteria and process to be used at different levels of abstraction. In essence, do they "scale-up" or "scale-down" to meet the "divide and conquer" intent at various levels? Do progressive aggregations of the same divisions reflect recognizable similarities? Restated differently, can the observer "zoom in" and "zoom out" and still retain a useful, relative perspective?

Effectiveness also relates to how the pieces combine to span the full range of concerns that the original concept entailed. Does the composition of the pieces effectively represent the concerns manifest in the whole (*wholeness* is the core goal)? Does the arrangement of pieces reflect an *unfolding*, an elaboration of structure that contributes to the explanation of the current relationships among the parts? An information systems modeler experiences and values this *choice* property as *stepwise refinement*.

3.2   Strong Centers to Cohesion

> Defines the way that a strong center requires a special field-like effect, created by other centers, as a primary source of its strength.

In models of information systems, *choices* in some modular form support one another in a collective. While their distinctiveness accents the coalescence of a single concept, they serve as constituents in the collective that accomplishes their corporate task of forming the whole. Well-defined *choices* reinforce the distributed contribution to the whole by removing the concerns central to each choice from those that surround it. In concert with the Levels of Scale property, Strong Centers brings focus to each *choice* as a clear, distinct, and discernible decision point in understanding and representing the whole. An information systems modeler experiences and values this *choice* property as *cohesion*.

3.3   Boundaries to Encapsulation

> The way that the field-like effect of a center is strengthened by the creation of a ring-like center, made of smaller centers that surround and intensify the first. The boundary also unites the center with the centers beyond it, thus strengthening it further.

In a collective of system *choices*, the distinctness and modularity of each individual *choice* combine much like the bounding function of a cellular membrane in biology. The boundary holds the module's *choice* (or collection of *choices*) separate and distinct while presenting the module as locally complete in itself to the system collective. Interfaces describe module cooperation at their boundaries. Interfaces breach the boundary that results from the single-minded focus of modules as strong *centers* to reveal the interaction they provide in the collective to support the whole. The module's separateness is balanced by a straightforward and intelligible description of "what" (defined by its interface) that *choice* does to cooperate with the collective around it. An information systems modeler experiences and values this *choice* property as *encapsulation* (or information hiding).

3.4   Alternating Repetition to Extensibility

> The way in which centers are strengthened when they repeat, by the insertion of other centers between the repeating ones.

When *choices* cooperate to achieve a result greater than their individual purpose, there is an amplification of *life*. The interoperation of modules with distinct purposes and functions fulfills the organizing principle of modularization. Furthermore, the participation of individual modules in different arrangements of cooperation reuses and retasks them to achieve more than a single purpose within the whole. The rearrangement in fact enables more function than the sum of the *choices*. Modules (*choices*) that are conceived to be reused and retasked offer the potential that a system's function can be expanded even after the modules have been crafted. An information systems modeler experiences and values this *choice* property as *extensibility*.

3.5   Positive Space to Modularization

> The way that a given center must draw its strength, in part, from the strength of other centers immediately adjacent to it in space.

In a system of modules reflecting the properties of Levels of Scale and Alternating Repetition as described earlier, some *choices* are crafted to always work in combination with others to achieve their collective purpose. Such a module depends at the outset of its conception on the subordinate cooperation of its neighbors. Its function is primarily to organize or coordinate the contribution of the subordinates to a purpose for which individually they may be ignorant; reflecting a separation of concerns. In this manner, the Levels of Scale can be extended to levels of management and dynamic direction toward the purpose of the whole. An information systems modeler experiences and values this *choice* property as *modularization*.

3.6   Good Shape to Correctness

> The way that the strength of a given center depends on its actual shape and the way this effect requires that even the shape, its boundary, and the space around it are made up of strong centers.

At this juncture in translating Alexander's concept of wholeness onto modeling information systems, Good Shape brings us to the point of examining the core of the concept, the essence of *choices* themselves. Together, the collective of *choices* constitutes the knowledge and understanding of the system under consideration.

Relevant, complete, clear, and concise are the characteristics of *choice* quality, its Good Shape. Relevant *choices* reflect the knowledge and understanding of stakeholders. If stakeholders are overlooked, uncooperative, or even ignorant, then knowledge and understanding will be incomplete. Clear *choices* communicate without doubt or confusion. Concise *choices* are free of extraneous or suspect knowledge or understanding.

Although all four characteristics are critical to quality, asserting concise *choices* may be the most difficult. This results from the individual human experience of stakeholders. To the extent that many if not most information systems are conceived to replace the physical or cognitive activities of humans, it is only natural for humans to describe their understanding of the system in terms of their own behavior in achieving its ends. The difficulty arises in the fact that some, if not most, of human behavior follows from habit or convenient, partially pre-existing *choices*, any or all of which are extraneous to defining the system goals, the essential whole. The difficulty lies not so much in the presence of these extraneous behaviors but in the failure to distinguish them from the germane, the essential understanding of the *choice* [2]. Left unchallenged, these accidents of implementation are mistaken for essential understanding and bore their way into the collective of *choices*, erroneously influencing the evolution of *choices* that follow. Although the pursuit of *wholeness* does not presume to guarantee perfection, to knowingly tolerate a discernible inferiority of *choice* denies respect for quality.

An information systems modeler experiences and values this *choice* property as *correctness*.

3.7 Local Symmetries to Transparency

The way that the intensity of a given center is increased by the extent to which other smaller centers that it contains are themselves arranged in locally symmetrical groups.

Discernible structure is an important part of clarity. The extent to which the composite structure of a *choice* is readily apparent enhances the observer's ability to understand and to recall the details of the given *choice*. This property interoperates with Levels of Scale and Positive Space to reinforce the perception of naturalness and order that exists in a cooperative grouping of *choices*.

Although there is merit in hiding information from clients of *choices* as in the discussion of Boundaries above, this does not extend to the modeler and builder. During operation and deployment, encapsulation promotes autonomy and separation of concerns. During conception and design, the purpose and composition of *choices* must enjoy transparency exposing the "patterns" and "weave" of their interconnectedness.

Simple symmetry like record or file structures regularize the collection and organization of information in implementation as well as design. More sophisticated mechanisms (e.g., inheritance and polymorphism) express symmetries that span the definition and the evolution of families of structure realizing a remarkable fidelity to Alexander's conception of *unfolding*. Symmetry is a core enabler of component reuse. An information systems modeler experiences and values this *choice* property as *transparency*.

3.8 Deep Interlock and Ambiguity to Composition of Function

The way in which the intensity of a given center can be increased when it is attached to nearby strong centers, through a third set of strong centers that ambiguously belong to both.

Choices that interoperate with superordinate *choices* to support a combined purpose tend to recede into the "shadows" as they perform their role largely anonymously. Acting as they do in Alternating Repetition, their combination forms new *choices* of function or behavior that subsume their individual identities. The fact that their local function may be reused or retasked renders their individual purposes somewhat ambiguous, as they are equally effective in multiple partnerships of whole support. An information systems modeler experiences and values this *choice* property as *composition of function*.

3.9 Contrast to Identity

The way that a center is strengthened by the sharpness of the distinction between its character and the character of surrounding centers.

There is no particular advantage in multiple *choices* accomplishing the same purpose. If two *choices* address the same purpose but in different manners, it would be beneficial to separate the "mannerism" from the "purpose" and merge the purposes where possible, thus eliminating redundancy of purpose and the potential for conflicting understanding (e.g., this property is the foundation for primary keys in data modeling). *Choices* that address the same purpose inevitably cause confusion either by the evidence of one absent the other or in the apparent conflict of their explanations within the whole. Clarity of distinctiveness diminishes confusion and simplifies learning and thus understanding. An information systems modeler experiences and values this *choice* property as *identity*.

3.10 Gradients to Scale

The way in which a center is strengthened by a graded series of different-sized centers that then "point" to the new center and intensify its field effect.

The practice of iterative decomposition (or iterative aggregation) has the effect of folding the understanding of a great amount of detail into a telescoping structure. That permits selective exhibition at whatever level of detail is appropriate. It is often the case that a great confidence in system understanding at one level of detail need not depend on complete exposure of the underlying levels. Layering is an important tool in complexity management in analysis, in design, in implementation, and in documentation of complex systems. Layering in the practice of modeling information systems can occur from various perspectives as well as various levels of module structure. Along with Levels of Scale, Gradients enable the elaboration of detail appropriate to the needs of particular observers. An information systems modeler experiences and values this *choice* property as *scale*.

3.11   Roughness to User Friendliness

> The way that the field effect of a given center draws its strength, necessarily, from irregularities in the sizes, shapes, and arrangements of other nearby centers.

In information systems, roughness reflects the perceptibility of access to a full range of system service via clearly defined interfaces. When the system is matched to the expectations of the stakeholders (particularly users), the range and granularity of interface options reflect the nature of the needs of the stakeholders to use the system in accomplishing their individual (and sometimes specialized) tasks. Although stakeholders may have widely varying needs for system interaction and patterns thereof, the system's interface texture should provide recognizable and collectively accessible services to their individual purposes. An information systems modeler experiences and values this *choice* property as *user friendliness*.

3.12   Echoes to Patterns

> The way that the strength of a given center depends on similarities of angle and orientation and systems of centers forming characteristic angles thus forming larger centers, among the centers it contains.

Despite the distinctiveness of each *choice* in a system, there should be a degree of harmony in the way those *choices* are exposed to stakeholders. Patterns of purpose found in collections of *choices* should be reflected in recognizable patterns of interface that reward familiarity in one context of interaction with ease of recognition in another. Similarities and parallels that reside in purpose should be reflected explicitly in interfaces. Standards, guidelines, and frameworks can be effective tools for exposing symmetry of purpose at the interfaces. An information systems modeler experiences and values this *choice* property as *patterns*.

3.13   The Void to Programmability

The way that the intensity of every center depends on the existence of a still place – an empty center – somewhere in its field.

The primary value in most information systems is not in the knowledge that is embedded in their construction (as dear as that may be), but rather it lies in the knowledge that may be gained from using one to resolve some stakeholder question after deployment. It is the question, the void of knowledge in the future, to which the system is directed that determines the system's value. The strength of a *choice* derives from the value of the question it will answer, the knowledge it will deliver, or the direction it indicates when it is applied to the intentions of the stakeholders.

From the user stakeholders' perspective, in computer software terms, this property is closely connected to the characteristic of programmability. Rather than being targeted to a single, narrow question or purpose, a programmable system provides its user with the means to dynamically retarget as the events of the world unfold in the user's time. The challenge of providing programmability in a *choice* is twofold: (1) to what range and extent should retargeting be enabled and (2) how much investment should be required of the user to accomplish the retargeting [3]? The developer stakeholders may wish to take *choices* that are specifically intended to support a range of purposes achieved primarily by aggregating various collections rather than multiplying *choices*. This might be described as "component-based design."

An information systems modeler experiences and values this *choice* property as *programmability*.

3.14   Simplicity and Inner Calm to Reliability

The way the strength of a center depends on its simplicity – on the process of reducing the number of different centers that exist in it, while increasing the strength of these centers to make them weigh more.

A *choice* achieves simplicity when it accomplishes its purpose without extraneous detail or embellishment. Although some details may be extraneous to the purpose at hand and appear to be benign, they still have an effect. To eschew extraneous detail is to avoid unwanted (unexpected) side effects that inevitably reveal themselves and foment confusion.

The baggage of extraneous detail or embellishment also leads to unwanted and unnecessary *choice* maintenance. Change is the enemy of calm. There is ample change in the real world. Why add to it for no good reason?

An information systems modeler experiences and values this *choice* property as *reliability*.

3.15   Not Separateness to Elegance

> The way the life and strength of a center depends on the extent to which that center is merged smoothly – sometimes even indistinguishably – with the centers that form its surroundings.

As this discussion of *wholeness* revolves around the concept of system *life*, it is only fitting to recognize that a system is a habitat for all the *choices* that compose it. The degree to which each *choice* "peacefully coexists" in the system depends on its contribution to the strength of the whole. In modeling, this can be affected by style, by perspective, by dialect, and even by tools above and beyond the core limitations of knowledge and understanding. As each *choice* is added into, deleted from, or modified in the collection, its radiating influence must be revisited, reconsidered, to assess the resulting effect on the whole. In the end, the difference between step and misstep in the unfolding process is whether the *wholeness* is increased or decreased. A decrease in *wholeness* regresses away from effectiveness and efficiency. An increase in *wholeness* progresses toward effectiveness and efficiency. Missteps will inevitably have to be undone if progress is to follow. An information systems modeler experiences and values this *choice* property as *elegance*.

3.16   Examining the Mapping from Center Properties to Choice Properties

Table 3.1 depicts Alexander's determination of property reinforcement [4]. A row depicts a property where each asterisk indicates those properties on which that row's property meaning or intensity relies. For example, Levels of Scale relies on Strong Centers, Boundaries, Good Shape, and Contrast. The final column is appended to recount the name of the *choice* property that corresponds to each of the *center* properties from the enumerated discussion above.

The translation of *center* property to *choice* property is necessarily an approximation. Alexander's language and precise terminology is intended for the academics and professionals of physical architecture. And as such, the metaphors and subtleties of that discipline are not perfectly congruent with information systems or computer science. The correlations are, however, compelling!

Whereas the mapping of Alexander's *center* properties to *choice* properties is interpretive, there can be no "proof of correctness" possible for the mapping in the mathematical or social sciences sense. However, convincing validation is attained by examining the internal consistency of the *choice* property interrelationships using Alexander's own matrix of property reliance in Table 3.1.

Table 3.1 Alexander's properties of *Centers* mapped to *Choice* properties

	Alexander's Property	1	2	3	4	5	6	7	8	9	10	11	12	13	14	15	Choice Property
1	Levels of Scale		*	*			*			*							Stepwise Refinement
2	Strong Centers			*			*		*	*			*			*	Cohesion
3	Boundaries		*		*			*	*	*	*						Encapsulation
4	Alternating Repetition		*			*	*		*	*						*	Extensibility
5	Positive Space	*	*	*			*	*		*		*		*			Modularization
6	Good Shape	*	*		*	*		*		*		*		*			Correctness
7	Local Symmetries	*				*				*			*				Transparency
8	Deep Interlock and Ambiguity				*	*				*		*	*			*	Composition of Function
9	Contrast			*		*			*		*			*		*	Identity
10	Gradients	*	*				*		*			*	*			*	Scale
11	Roughness		*			*	*			*				*		*	User Friendliness
12	Echoes	*				*	*			*	*					*	Patterns
13	The Void	*		*		*		*		*				*			Programmability
14	Simplicity and Inner Calm					*	*					*	*			*	Reliability
15	Not Separateness			*		*			*		*	*		*	*		Elegance

Alexander explains the properties and interdependencies depicted in Table 3.1 over a complete volume of his treatise on The Nature of Order. (The reader is encouraged to explore Alexander's explanations firsthand.) In lieu of that level of detail, it is instructive to expand the representation of the table's contents and consider how each property interrelates to the others by enumerating the related properties. It is also interesting to see how the *choice* property mappings also intimate interesting nuances of design. Table 3.2 "unpacks" the encoding of Table 3.1 transcribing it into words and replacing the asterisks with their corresponding *center* properties and *choice* properties.

The reader may wish to pause at this point to consider the terms and relationships, perhaps reviewing their own experience of building information systems to consider if the mappings offered here capture any of their own philosophy or insight in answering the question, "How do you assess a good model, a great design?"

Table 3.2 Expanded mapping of properties of *Centers* to *Choice* properties

	Alexander's Property	Supported by:	Choice Property	Supported by:
1	Levels of Scale	Strong Centers Boundaries Good Shape Contrast	Stepwise Refinement	Cohesion Encapsulation Correctness Identity
2	Strong Centers	Alternating Repetition Local Symmetries Contrast Gradients The Void Not Separateness	Cohesion	Extensibility Transparency Identity Scale Programmability Elegance

3	Boundaries	Strong Centers
		Alternating Repetition
		Local Symmetries
		Deep Interlock and
		   Ambiguity
		Contrast
		Gradients
			Encapsulation	Cohesion
				Extensibility
				Transparency
				Composition of
				   Function
				Identity
				Scale

4	Alternating Repetition	Strong Centers
		Positive Space
		Good Shape
		Deep Interlock and
		   Ambiguity
		Contrast
		Not Separateness
			Extensibility	Cohesion
				Modularization
				Correctness
				Composition of
				   Function
				Identity
				Elegance

5	Positive Space	Levels of Scale Strong Centers Boundaries Good Shape Local Symmetries Contrast Roughness The Void	Modularization	Stepwise Refinement Cohesion Encapsulation Correctness Transparency Identity User Friendliness Programmability

6	Good Shape	Levels of Scale
		Strong Centers
		Positive Space
		Good Shape
		Deep Interlock and
		   Ambiguity
		Gradients
		Echoes
		Simplicity and
		   Inner Calm
			Correctness	Stepwise Refinement
				Cohesion
				Modularization
				Correctness
				Composition of
				   Function
				Scale
				Patterns
				Reliability

7	Local Symmetries	Levels of Scale Positive Space Contrast The Void	Transparency	Stepwise Refinement Modularization Identity Programmability
8	Deep Interlock and Ambiguity	Alternating Repetition Positive Space Contrast Roughness Echoes The Void	Composition of Function	Extensibility Modularization Identity User Friendliness Patterns Programmability

Table 3.2 (continued)

	Alexander's Property	Supported by:	Choice Property	Supported by:

9	Contrast	Boundaries
		Positive Space
		Deep Interlock and
		  Ambiguity
		Gradients
		The Void
		Not Separateness
			Identity	Encapsulation
				Modularization
				Composition of
				  Function
				Scale
				Programmability
				Elegance

10	Gradients	Levels of Scale Strong Centers Local Symmetries Contrast Roughness Echoes Not Separateness	Scale	Stepwise Refinement Cohesion Transparency Identity User Friendliness Patterns Elegance
11	Roughness	Strong Centers Positive Space Good Shape Gradients Simplicity and Inner Calm Not Separateness	User Friendliness	Cohesion Modularization Correctness Scale Reliability Elegance
12	Echoes	Levels of Scale Good Shape Local Symmetries Gradients Roughness Not Separateness	Patterns	Stepwise Refinement Correctness Transparency Scale User Friendliness Elegance
13	The Void	Levels of Scale Boundaries Positive Space Local Symmetries Contrast Simplicity and Inner Calm	Programmability	Stepwise Refinement Encapsulation Modularization Transparency Identity Reliability
14	Simplicity and Inner Calm	Good Shape Local Symmetries Echoes The Void Not Separateness	Reliability	Correctness Transparency Patterns Programmability Elegance

15	Not Separateness	Boundaries
		Positive Space
		Deep Interlock and
		  Ambiguity
		Gradients
		Roughness
		The Void
		Simplicity and Inner
		  Calm
			Elegance	Encapsulation
				Modularization
				Composition of
				  Function
				Scale
				User Friendliness
				Programmability
				Reliability

References

1. Waguespack LJ Jr, "Hammers, Nails, Windows, Doors and Teaching Great Design," *Information Systems Education Journal*, 6 (45). http://isedj.org/6/45/. ISSN: 1545-679X, 2008. (A preliminary version appears in *The Proceedings of ISECON 2007*: §3324. ISSN: 1542-7382.)
2. Brooks FP., "No Silver Bullet: Essence and Accidents of Software Engineering," Computer, Vol. 20, No. 4 (April 1987) pp 10–19.
3. Waguespack LJ Jr and Schiano WT, 2003 "Component-Based IS Architecture," In IS Management Handbook, 8th Edition, Chapter 42, Auerbach, CRC Press LLC, Boca Raton, Florida, pp 531–543.
4. Alexander C, The Nature of Order An Essay on the Art of Building and the Nature of the Universe: Book I - The Phenomenon of Life, Berkeley, CA: The Center for Environmental Structure, 2002, p 238.

Chapter 4
Achieving Versus Observing Strength in Choice Properties

None of the 15 properties can be experienced completely in isolation from all the others. This is also true in assessing the property strength of any particular *choice*. The properties always combine in the field-effect of *choice* strength. This largely proceeds from Alexander's own explanation of properties supporting properties. In this regard, it is perhaps more natural to think of the *choice* properties as something that are primarily "discovered" or "witnessed" through inspection of a pre-existing system or structure. In understanding the properties of *centers* or *choices*, the first and most natural experience is observation.

The order in nature that these properties exhibit (and explain) results from eons of evolution, the trial and error of natural selection (animal, vegetable, mineral, and cosmic), that over countless centuries has weeded out those structures and relationships that do not possess the order that permits survival; those that do not exhibit sustainable order.

The task at hand is to determine if sustainable order through *living structure* can be achieved through engineering rather than eons of trial and error. This chapter explores achieving strength in the 15 *choice* properties by design through the actions of modeling. The 15 *choice* properties along with their antecedent *center* properties are again recounted (see Table 4.1) with the addition of action verbs that summarize and characterize the formative process applied through a *choice* to achieve property strength. A terse description of the action in this context accompanies each verb.

In the sections that follow, each verb is explored to characterize its impact on *choice* formation. Each property is accompanied by its supporting properties list. The reader is again reminded that the properties are not achievable in isolation and that these modeling action verbs regularly occur in combination and cooperation.

4.1 Stepwise Refinement (To Elaborate)

Stepwise Refinement: to develop or present (a theory, policy, or system) in detail supported by:

L.J. Waguespack, *Thriving Systems Theory and Metaphor-Driven Modeling*,
DOI 10.1007/978-1-84996-302-2_4, © Springer-Verlag London Limited 2010

Table 4.1 Modeling actions attributable to achieving choice properties

	Alexander's Property	Choice Property	Modeling Action	Plausible Action Definition
1	Levels of Scale	Stepwise Refinement	Elaborate	Develop or present (a theory, policy, or system) in detail
2	Strong Centers	Cohesion	Factor	Express as a product of factors
3	Boundaries	Encapsulation	Encapsulate	Enclose the essential features of something succinctly by a protective coating or membrane
4	Alternating Repetition	Extensibility	Extend	Render something capable of expansion in scope, effect, or meaning
5	Positive Space	Modularization	Modularize	Employing or involving a module or modules as the basis of design or construction
6	Good Shape	Correctness	Align	Put (things) into correct or appropriate relative positions
7	Local Symmetries	Transparency	Expose	Reveal the presence of (a quality or feeling)
8	Deep Interlock and Ambiguity	Composition of Function	Assemble	Fit together the separate component parts of (a machine or other object)
9	Contrast	Identity	Identify	Establish or indicate who or what (someone or something) is
10	Gradients	Scale	Focus	(Of a person or their eyes) Adapt to the prevailing level of light [abstraction] and become able to see clearly
11	Roughness	User Friendliness	Accommodate	Fit in with the wishes or needs of
12	Echoes	Patterns	Pattern	Give a regular or intelligible form to
13	The Void	Programmability	Generalize	Make or become more widely or generally applicable
14	Simplicity and Inner Calm	Reliability	Normalize	Make something more normal, which typically means conforming to some regularity or rule
15	Not Separateness	Elegance	Coordinate	Bring the different elements of (a complex activity or organization) into a relationship that is efficient or harmonious

Cohesion: to express as a product of factors

Encapsulation: to enclose the essential features of something succinctly by a protective coating or membrane

Correctness: to put (things) into correct or appropriate relative positions

Identity: to establish or indicate who or what (someone or something) is

Strengthening the *choice* property of *stepwise refinement* is the exposure of system features in digestible increments in a spiral of incremental explanation as in a pedagogy. The model designer's task is to deliver a succession of reinforcing representations that explain the parts within an outline of the whole, an elaboration of system elements that shapes the observers' understanding consistent with the system's stakeholder intentions, and an exposition of structure as parts assembled to form the whole. In a sense, strengthening this property is analogous to revealing the observable refinements evidenced in evolution – a succession of steps that has led it now to what it is.

4.2   Cohesion (To Factor)

Cohesion: to express as a product of factors supported by:

Extensibility: to render something capable of expansion in scope, effect, or meaning

Transparency: to reveal the presence of (a quality or feeling)

Identity: to establish or indicate who or what (someone or something) is

Scale: to (of a person or their eyes) adapt to the prevailing level of light [abstraction] and become able to see clearly

Programmability: to make or become more widely or generally applicable

Elegance: to bring the different elements of (a complex activity or organization) into a relationship that is efficient or harmonious

Strengthening the *choice* property of *cohesion* results from factorization that reveals/defines the fundamental system features. The model designer's tasks are to identify the fundamental, to distill the idea, to isolate the concept, to separate and distinguish the part, to name the primitive, to minimize coupling, and to define the elemental component. And in so doing, the model designer renders the *choice* individually and distinguishably complete in its own purpose.

4.3   Encapsulation (To Encapsulate)

Encapsulation: to enclose the essential features of something succinctly by a protective coating or membrane supported by:

Cohesion: to express as a product of factors

Extensibility: to render something capable of expansion in scope, effect, or meaning

Transparency: to reveal the presence of (a quality or feeling)

Composition of Function: to fit together the separate component parts of (a machine or other object)

Identity: to establish or indicate who or what (someone or something) is

Scale: to (of a person or their eyes) adapt to the prevailing level of light [abstraction] and become able to see clearly

Strengthening the *choice* property of *encapsulation* results from identifying and insulating essential features while controlling access through disciplined, contractual interfaces. The model designer's tasks are to protect, to compartmentalize, to relegate, to steward, to cast, to recast, to virtualize, to package, to mask, to portray, to "component-ize," to characterize, to abstract, and to hold inviolate. And in so doing, not only are the internals "protected," but also the *choice*'s clients are freed from any obligatory knowledge of the details of the *choice*'s internals.

4.4 Extensibility (To Render Extendable)

Extensibility: to render something capable of expansion in scope, effect, or meaning supported by:

Cohesion: to express as a product of factors

Modularization: to employ or involve a module or modules as the basis of design or construction

Correctness: to put (things) into correct or appropriate relative positions

Composition of Function: to fit together the separate component parts of (a machine or other object)

Identity: to establish or indicate who or what (someone or something) is

Elegance: to bring the different elements of (a complex activity or organization) into a relationship that is efficient or harmonious

Strengthening the *choice* property of *extensibility* results in model features so crafted that extended functionality or additional features may be added with a minimum of cost or disruption to the whole. The model designer's tasks are to expose the "common denominators" of feature functionality, to sharpen the "articulation points" that accentuate the "creases" in the *unfolding* structure/behavior of the model, and to expose the potential for "partnering" among the model *choices*. And in so doing, the *choice* represents not only the achievement of purpose in the present but is also poised to achieve an evolving purpose in the future.

4.5 Modularization (To Modularize)

Modularization: to employ or involve a module or modules as the basis of design or construction supported by:

Stepwise Refinement: to develop or present (a theory, policy, or system) in detail

Cohesion: to express as a product of factors

Encapsulation: to enclose the essential features of something succinctly by a protective coating or membrane

Correctness: to put (things) into correct or appropriate relative positions

Transparency: to reveal the presence of (a quality or feeling)

Identity: to establish or indicate who or what (someone or something) is

User Friendliness: to fit in with the wishes or needs of

Programmability: to make or become more widely or generally applicable

Strengthening the *choice* property of *modularization* is to partition and associate system knowledge that facilitates "divide and conquer" problem-solving or the segmented exposure of system features aligned to the stakeholders' intention. The model designer's tasks are to compartmentalize, to aggregate, and to express the system as wholes and parts. And in so doing, the whole is revealed through "bite-sized" pieces that promote comprehension and facilitate management.

4.6   Correctness (To Align)

Correctness: to put (things) into correct or appropriate relative positions supported by:

Stepwise Refinement: to develop or present (a theory, policy, or system) in detail

Cohesion: to express as a product of factors

Modularization: to employ or involve a module or modules as the basis of design or construction

Correctness: to put (things) into correct or appropriate relative positions

Composition of Function: to fit together the separate component parts of (a machine or other object)

Scale: to (of a person or their eyes) adapt to the prevailing level of light [abstraction] and become able to see clearly

Patterns: to give a regular or intelligible form to

Reliability: to make something more normal, which typically means conforming to some regularity or rule

Strengthening the *choice* property of *correctness* results from relevant, complete, clear, and concise representation of the stakeholders' intentions in model features. The model designer's tasks are to represent stakeholder intentions faithfully, to reflect them consistently, to eschew contradictions, to reflect expectations, to align with beliefs, to satisfy the stakeholders' intentions, and to effectively model concerns. And in so doing, the *choice* reflects "truthfully" the stakeholders' intentions and forms a solid foundation on which a subsequent elaboration may proceed with fidelity.

4.7 Transparency (To Expose)

Transparency: to reveal the presence of (a quality or feeling) supported by:

Stepwise Refinement: to develop or present (a theory, policy, or system) in detail

Modularization: to employ or involve a module or modules as the basis of design or construction

Identity: to establish or indicate who or what (someone or something) is

Programmability: to make or become more widely or generally applicable

Strengthening the *choice* property of *transparency* exposes the intention rendered in a model clearly and thus eschews obfuscation. The designer's tasks are to reveal, to render visible, to portray as to interpret, to disclose, to shed light, to unfold, to uncover, to lay bare, to bear witness to the stakeholders' intentions, to be true to those intentions, to make self-evident, to make self-explanatory, to publish, and to promote the underlying intentions. And to this end, the model designer avoids obscuring stakeholder intentions in either the elaboration of a *choice* or the application of extensions to it.

4.8 Composition of Function (To Assemble)

Composition of Function: to fit together the separate component parts of (a machine or other object) supported by:

Extensibility: to render something capable of expansion in scope, effect, or meaning

Modularization: to employ or involve a module or modules as the basis of design or construction

Identity: to establish or indicate who or what (someone or something) is

User Friendliness: to fit in with the wishes or needs of

Patterns: to give a regular or intelligible form to

Programmability: to make or become more widely or generally applicable

Strengthening the *choice* property of *composition of function* exploits the constituent potential of model *choices* combining them as individual contributors to a new and distinctive configuration. The designer's task is to build, to compose, to manufacture, to piece together, to assemble, to construct, to combine, to package, to fabricate, to erect, to connect, or to join. And in so doing, the designer exercises the constituent parts' potential deposited through *extensibility* and/or *programmability* by producing a whole that is "greater than the sum of its parts."

4.9 Identity (To Identify)

Identity: to establish or indicate who or what (someone or something) is supported by:

Encapsulation: to enclose the essential features of something succinctly by a protective coating or membrane

Modularization: to employ or involve a module or modules as the basis of design or construction

Composition of Function: to fit together the separate component parts of (a machine or other object)

Scale: to (of a person or their eyes) adapt to the prevailing level of light [abstraction] and become able to see clearly

Programmability: to make or become more widely or generally applicable

Elegance: to bring the different elements of (a complex activity or organization) into a relationship that is efficient or harmonious

Strengthening the *choice* property of *identity* results when a modeling element is named and its existence is recognized. The naming of model elements constitutes the vocabulary describing and explaining the whole. To "name" something is to "know" it, to distinguish it among the rest, to justify its individual existence, to recognize its distinctiveness, to carve out a subset of the universe and label it, and to collect its attributes and package them as a definite concept. To establish element identity is at the core of language; that a "name" can take the place of all that is known about an element and carry that knowledge through an explanation or analysis. A "name" may be completely distinguishing or categorical, respectively, expressing either individuality or a shared context. In any case, a "name" is a handle with which to grasp and carry a concept within a conversation, be it noun (subject), verb (predicate), or adjective (modifier).

4.10   Scale (To Focus)

Scale: to (of a person or their eyes) adapt to the prevailing level of light [abstraction] and become able to see clearly supported by:

Stepwise Refinement: to develop or present (a theory, policy, or system) in detail

Cohesion: to express as a product of factors

Transparency: to reveal the presence of (a quality or feeling)

Identity: to establish or indicate who or what (someone or something) is

User Friendliness: to fit in with the wishes or needs of

Patterns: to give a regular or intelligible form to

Elegance: to bring the different elements of (a complex activity or organization) into a relationship that is efficient or harmonious

Strengthening the *choice* property of *scale* results from the imposition of a telescoping sense of focus that may be directed to an observer's purpose and renders in clarity the system features relevant to that purpose. The model designer's tasks are to direct attention, to highlight, to draw attention to, to lend perspective, to acquaint, to draw parallels with, to contextualize, to put into perspective, to lead an observer through the *unfolding*, to familiarize, to introduce, to bring into focus, to zero in, to target, and to "point to." And in so doing, the model designer provides a telescoping granularity of comprehensibility to suit the requirements of a variety of observers.

4.11   User Friendliness (To Accommodate)

User Friendliness: to fit in with the wishes or needs of supported by:

Cohesion: to express as a product of factors

Modularization: to employ or involve a module or modules as the basis of design or construction

Correctness: to put (things) into correct or appropriate relative positions

Scale: to (of a person or their eyes) adapt to the prevailing level of light [abstraction] and become able to see clearly

Reliability: to make something more normal, which typically means conforming to some regularity or rule

Elegance: to bring the different elements of (a complex activity or organization) into a relationship that is efficient or harmonious

Strengthening the *choice* property of *user friendliness* results when the system's features accommodate the stakeholders' intention. The model designer's tasks are to promote comfort, to foster self-evidence, to facilitate recognition, to promote explicit consistency, to distinguish among differences, to represent the familiar, to satisfy the observer, to reinforce the connectedness of observer and the system, and to reinforce the observer's sense of the system's conformance with his or her belief. And in so doing, the model *choice* appears to the stakeholder as convenient and completely expected.

4.12   Patterns (To Pattern)

Patterns: to give a regular or intelligible form to supported by:

Stepwise Refinement: to develop or present (a theory, policy, or system) in detail

Correctness: to put (things) into correct or appropriate relative positions

Transparency: to reveal the presence of (a quality or feeling)

Scale: to (of a person or their eyes) adapt to the prevailing level of light [abstraction] and become able to see clearly

User Friendliness: to fit in with the wishes or needs of

Elegance: to bring the different elements of (a complex activity or organization) into a relationship that is efficient or harmonious

Strengthening the *choice* property of *patterns* results from discovery and/or designation of explicit similarity and difference. The model designer's tasks are to characterize similarity, to expose repetition, to map consistency, to reuse the familiar, to prescribe the evolution, to weave, to interlock, to establish a rhythm, to facilitate a path of lesser resistance, to foreshadow, to anticipate, to lead, to invite, to predict, to train, and to condition. And in so doing, the *pattern* strength of the *choice* both invites and conditions the observers to consider reuse.

4.13   Programmability (To Generalize)

Programmability: to make or become more widely or generally applicable supported by:

Stepwise Refinement: to develop or present (a theory, policy, or system) in detail

Encapsulation: to enclose the essential features of something succinctly by a protective coating or membrane

Modularization: to employ or involve a module or modules as the basis of design or construction

Transparency: to reveal the presence of (a quality or feeling)

Identity: to establish or indicate who or what (someone or something) is

Reliability: to make something more normal, which typically means conforming to some regularity or rule

Strengthening the *choice* property of *programmability* is to distinguish that which is the option from that which is the rule such that the range of options complement the rule. The model designer's tasks are to formalize a language of versatility, to expose the versatility of, to control the exposure of that versatility, to regularize the alternatives of, abstract the interface of, to delay the binding of, to extend an interface's representation beyond a "binary switch" toward a "conversational dialogue." And in so doing, the options become extensions of the rule that give flexibility to the stakeholders' application of system features and to their perception of the "problem-solving" tasks using it.

4.14   Reliability (To Normalize)

Reliability: to make something more normal, which typically means conforming to some regularity or rule supported by:

Correctness: to put (things) into correct or appropriate relative positions

Transparency: to reveal the presence of (a quality or feeling)

Patterns: to give a regular or intelligible form to

Programmability: to make or become more widely or generally applicable

Elegance: to bring the different elements of (a complex activity or organization) into a relationship that is efficient or harmonious

Strengthening the *choice* property of *reliability* results from an economy of model features limited to the stakeholders' intentions devoid of extraneous embellishments. The model designer's tasks are to regularize, to bring into conformance, to align with stakeholder rules, to represent as aligned with rules, to promote predictability, to render explainable, to conform to the expected, and to eschew the unexpected. And in so doing, the *choice* represents "the truth, the whole truth and nothing but the truth." In the truest sense, *reliability* means that "you get what you bargain for" without unexpected complications or entanglements.

4.15   Elegance (To Coordinate)

Elegance: to bring the different elements of (a complex activity or organization) into a relationship that is efficient or harmonious supported by:

Encapsulation: to enclose the essential features of something succinctly by a protective coating or membrane

Modularization: to employ or involve a module or modules as the basis of design or construction

Composition of Function: to fit together the separate component parts of (a machine or other object)

Scale: to (of a person or their eyes) adapt to the prevailing level of light [abstraction] and become able to see clearly

User Friendliness: to fit in with the wishes or needs of

Programmability: to make or become more widely or generally applicable

Reliability: to make something more normal, which typically means conforming to some regularity or rule

Strengthening the *choice* property of *elegance* results from coordinating *choices* to produce an arrangement where each mutually reinforces the other as they fuse into the unifying intention of the whole. The designer's tasks are to harmonize, to orchestrate, to make whole, to complete, and to render the system acceptable by validating the stakeholders' intentions through the system's features. And in so doing, the *choice* resonates with the stakeholders' conception and expectation of its place and role in the whole, which satisfies their needs.

4.16   Modeling Actions: Syntax and Semantics

It can be noted that several of the action verbs discussed here find direct syntactic correlations in dialects of modeling and programming languages commonly used in system development. In many instances, the language design goals and objectives are bent specifically to facilitate the ease of achieving these various properties in system description.

Specific modeling paradigms often favor a particular subset of the 15 properties in their representational philosophy. This makes some modeling tasks more or less attuned to promoting that subset of properties. The less favored properties are usually not prohibited by a paradigm's nature, but require additional effort on the part of the modeler or designer to achieve them. In Chapters 11 and 12, this phenomenon of property favoritism is illustrated in an exercise of describing the development of *living structure* using, respectively, the object-oriented and relational paradigms of information system modeling.

In any case, the "tools" provided in any particular dialect's syntax and semantics are indeed only implements that may be applied through enlightened consciousness to achieve the stakeholders' intentions in a system of *living structure*. The "tools" cannot compensate in any way for a weak or absent consciousness of the stakeholders' intentions. The next chapter introduces the process of *unfolding* that Christopher Alexander describes as enabling the building of *life* into products of architecture. With that basis, the chapter explores the adaptation of his process to building *life* into information systems.

Chapter 5
Building *Life* into Information Systems

Just as Christopher Alexander's ultimate goal is to enlighten architects and improve their products for society's sake, incorporating the *wholeness* theory into systems development can have similar benefits to society's information systems. The following discussion explores an approach informed by the theory of *wholeness* and *life*.

5.1 A Life-Infusing Process for Building Information Systems

One of Alexander's primary arguments is that process is the key to the success of bringing about systems with *life*. He sums up his argument as follows:

> Our current view of architecture rests on too little awareness of becoming as the most essential feature of the building process. Architects are much too concerned with the design of the world (its static structure) and not yet concerned enough with the design of the generative processes that create the world (its dynamic structure). [1]

The building of a house or office building or an information system is the result of thousands (perhaps tens of thousands) of decisions. Each of these decisions may result in more or less *life* in the resulting structure. Any hope that the product achieves significant *life* depends on the compounding effects of good decision after good decision. Alexander argues that good decisions form a stepwise *unfolding* where each transformation step intentionally attempts to enhance the whole by applying a transformation that intensifies one or more of the 15 properties of *centers* forming the *wholeness*. A transformation can change the number of *center*(s) (*choice*(s)) or alter the property(s) of the existing one(s). The key is continuous awareness of the 15 properties and how each transformation affects the *life* of the whole.

5.2   Applying Alexander's Generative Building Process

Christopher Alexander's theory and philosophy of building to achieve *life* through a structure-preserving transformation process resonates across the breadth of software engineering principles that have evolved over the past several decades. More importantly, it resonates with the more recent focus of attention on systems as reflected in business models, business process models, and business process reengineering independent of software design or programming. In a fundamental sense, Alexander's approach focuses on the "why" of the building process. He continuously redirects decision-making energy to the question, "How does each decision increase *life* in the system by fulfilling the stakeholders' evolving concerns?" and "What does *life* mean to these stakeholders?"

Much of the progress of systems and software engineering has served to make systems more "objectively" sound, but is that sufficient if their "subjective" soundness is in question? Alexander argues that when the "why" is left separate from the "what" and the "how," the system may work but it will lack *life*. Alexander explains that "lack of *life*" as "... ways in which the (system) fails to do what it is supposed to do, fails to meet the needs of the people who use it or is more awkward, more annoying, less useful, than it is supposed to be" [1, p. 198]. Alexander's theoretical and philosophical conception of building for *life* offers a fixative, applying proven software engineering principles that achieve effective and efficient systems not only in "objectivity," the "mechanics of system implementation," but also in "subjectivity," the harmony with the "why" of the system's stakeholders. This "glue" is not a new principle, but rather it is a clarified vision of where, when, how, and why to incorporate software engineering principles in the system-building process. This "clarified vision" does not directly require that developers change what they do to build information systems, but rather to change how they think about what they do.

5.3   Complexity and the Improbability of Working Systems

The statistics of system reliability readily show that the multiplication of parts exponentially decreases the probability that the whole will be reliable – unless there is a compensating exponential increase in the reliability of each individual part. So how then is it possible to engineer a working system with more than a few dozen parts? Consider, for example, that to produce a system of 100 parts with a 90% reliability, each part must be at least 99.89% reliable. Put another way, if the system were to be expected to perform correctly 9 out of 10 times, each and every part would have to fail fewer than 11 times out of every 10,000 tests! Then, how is it that in the natural world all around us there are working biological and ecological systems with literally millions of parts? Alexander's answer to this question is generated structures.

> All the well-ordered complex systems we know in the world, all those anyway that we view as highly successful, are GENERATED structures, not fabricated structures. [1, p. 180]

The first definition offered by the New Oxford American Dictionary, 2nd Ed., for "fabricate" is "to falsify, to fake, cook; invent, make up" as if to emphasize that building in any other way than generating may result in the appearance of the desired outcome, but will at best only achieve an illusion of a viable system.

Alexander notes in reference to information systems that some computer scientists have proudly told him that computer programs are the most complex objects ever designed by humans. He responds as follows.

> If indeed the programs are so complex, then it is likely that they, too, will be potentially subject to hundreds of thousands, perhaps millions of egregious mistakes of adaptation. Here I am not only talking about "bugs" – failures which stop a program from running altogether. I am talking about mistakes of adaptation, ways in which the program fails to do what it is supposed to do, fails to meet the needs of the people who use it or is more awkward, more annoying, less useful, than it is supposed to be. ...[I]t is fair to say that truly successful programs can only be generated; and that the way forward in the next decades, towards programs with highly adapted human performance, will be through programs which are generated through unfolding, in some fashion comparable to what I have described for buildings. [1, p. 198]

So what about complexity; how is it overcome? The complexity that defeats comprehension does not result from the number of parts found in the construction or the number of steps that make up a process. The complexity that defeats comprehension results from the lack of a discernible path in the *unfolding* system structure. For an observer to understand a system, they must be able to "see" how the parts interrelate and interoperate in the structure or process. More succinctly, how the parts contribute to the *wholeness* of the system must be evident. Exposing this "path" has always been at the foundation of problem-solving mechanisms and techniques evolved over the ages to deal with complexity. Consider two common examples.

Divide and conquer, a ubiquitous problem-solving mechanism, permits the problem-solver to modularize the understanding of the problem by partitioning the overall issue into pieces that either permit creative solution of each piece by brute force or facilitate reformulating the piece to fit a pre-existing solution that may be applied "off the shelf." Another example, encapsulation, is a technique whereby each partitioned piece is so formulated as to have as little as possible cross-dependency with any other piece, thereby allowing the pieces (and their solutions) to be addressed with minimal interaction. Both these mechanisms for controlling complexity clearly focus on the *choices* as *centers* in the structure and manage the introduction and arrangement of new *choices* to intensify the properties of *strong centers*, *boundaries*, *good shape*, *contrast*, and *not separateness*. The structure of the whole *unfolds* to clear and visible purpose.

5.4 Generated Structures: Top-Down Versus Bottom-Up

"Generated not fabricated" has far-reaching implications for the process of constructing systems with "*living structure*." Alexander explains:

> The key to complex adaptation in a generated structure lies in the concept of differentiation. This is a process of dividing and differentiating a whole to get the parts, rather than adding parts together to get a whole.
>
> In a structure which is differentiated, the structure will not, in general, be made by small piecemeal acts happening in random order. Rather, each step creates the context for the next step in the whole and allows the process as a whole to lay down, next, what has to be laid down next in order for an orderly unfolding to occur and to allow a simple and coherent form to arise in which, nevertheless, all the important small details are done just right. [1, p. 197]

Alexander describes the generative process as top-down rather than bottom-up. Each decision from choice to choice to choice in the overall process of building must be advised by the alignment of its focus with the whole. The whole is never eclipsed by the detail of any particular choice – this is the property Not Separateness. Bottom-up may be a useful technique in developing an understanding of the problem domain to be addressed, but it is at best an antecedent to the modeling and building process. The process that builds systems with living structure must begin with a consciousness of the whole and stepwise elaborate that vision with detail – unfolding that vision as countless implementation details (*choices*) addressing the problem domain.

Alexander's theory of building *living structure* is not the first to advocate top-down as a pre-eminent approach to system design. Software development gurus of the "structured programming" era ardently advocated for this approach. Wirth [2], Mills [3], Parnas [4], Boehm [5], and Brooks [6] (among others) espoused a top-down emphasis in software design. Their arguments focus on computer software and they do not purport to identify underlying "laws of nature" as Alexander does. But their basic conviction agrees with Alexander and reinforces the proposition that Alexander is uncovering underlying, fundamental principles of effective information system design.

5.5 Accident of Implementation: Threat to System Life

An outgrowth of Alexander's philosophy of system building is that the result must form a continuity with the surrounding domain. That continuity spans both the immediate static interrelationships of the various parts and also the dynamic continuity with the past and future of the system. This is the essence of *life* that Alexander refers to as *living structure*. It is a system that accounts and responds both to the immediate needs of the acts of living that it supports and is informed and honors the history of those needs while anticipating the evolution of those needs into the future. Alexander puts it this way:

> This is a startling and new conception of ethics and aesthetics. It describes good structure as a structure which has unfolded "well," through these transformations, without violating the structure that exists. The structure we know [...] as living structure, is just that kind of structure which has unfolded smoothly and naturally, arising step by step from what exists, preserving the structure of what exists and allowing the "new" to grow in the most natural way as a development from the structure of "what is." This startling view provides us with a view of

ethics and aesthetics that dignifies our respect for what exists and treasures that which grows from this respect. It views with disfavor only that which emerges arbitrarily, without respect for what exists and provides a vision of the world as a horn of shimmering plenty in which the "new" grows unceasingly from the structure that exists around us already. [7]

Alexander's vision applies in virtually the identical fashion to information systems as he applies it to houses, buildings, and cities. The core of efficiency and effectiveness emanates from the fidelity that system architects achieve in capturing and reflecting the culture of the problem domain and the intention of the stakeholders in conducting their enterprise within that domain. The inefficiencies and ineffectiveness of information systems lie in the propagation of arbitrary structures that are not grounded in the culture of the domain or the intention of the stakeholders. These problems are exacerbated when these arbitrary structures are not recognized as arbitrary. Arbitrary *choices* stem from three main sources: weak domain analysis, misunderstood practice, and implementation decisions.

Arbitrary *choices* arise from a lack of understanding because of an ineffective study of the problem domain. In any problem-solving approach, it is crucial to identify the relevant domain characteristics that influence effectiveness and efficiency. This two-phase task, the identification of recognizable problem domain characteristics and then the assessment/assignment of relative relevance, can be economically challenging. False economy leads to insufficient problem domain research and the introduction of arbitrary *choices* perhaps more often than do misunderstood practice or implementation decisions.

Stakeholders are not always well informed. They are very familiar with their own behavior in the problem domain, but are not always conscious of why they do what they do or how they do it. Misunderstandings commonly occur in process settings where common practice is misconstrued as stakeholder *choice* when it is just habit! "That's the way it's done." is poor evidence that a *choice* is not arbitrary.

Arbitrary *choices* also arise from the decisions to use various techniques or technologies in implementing a system. In this case, a *choice* becomes arbitrary not because its inclusion is careless or unconsidered but because it is one of the multiple options that could have been used and the reason for selecting this option is not made explicit. As such, the reason for selection (or the fact that there were options) does not become an explicit matter of understanding in the structure rationale moving forward. The arbitrary *choice*, the *accident of implementation*, persists as if it was a necessity determined by the stakeholders rather than an option selected to make sense at a certain point in history. Understanding why things are as they are is fundamental to the *life-preserving generative process*.

5.6 Peripheral Vision in the "Mind's Eye"

If generating and maintaining *wholeness* intact depends on structure-preserving process steps, the very earliest steps in any design activity critically influence whether there will be a quality outcome. Alexander states:

Design itself, of course, is a process and, as in every other process, the quality of what is designed will flow from the quality of this process. ... As any designer will tell you, it is the first steps in a design process which count for most. The first few strokes, which create the form, carry within them the destiny of the rest. ...

In the early stage of design we must concentrate, of course, on broad structure, on the emergent structure of the whole. [7, p. 256]

Realizing "the emergent structure of the whole" depends on a process of eliciting, distilling, coalescing, and communicating (and often creating) a composite understanding acceptable to a stakeholder community. Each stakeholder can present a distinct and potentially contradictory perspective of "reality" – what each experiences. Each depicts the "truth" as they see it. Each represents an aspect that will shape the assessment of "success" in the finally rendered model(s). The confluence (sometimes collision) of stakeholder experiences results in a formidable challenge for the modeler whose task is to compose and communicate a cogent and effective image of "the" system.

How can the modeler deal with distinct and/or contradictory aspects and yet approach clarity? How should he/she "think" about the "reality" expressed by stakeholders to fashion a unified image of the system in his/her "mind's eye?" What are the "marks" or "shapes" that form the modeler's vision of the system? What conception or cognitive structure can contain both what the stakeholders know and what they assume about the system and yet can be suitably unfolded toward a useful, satisfying product? To address this challenge, we must ask how humans understand and in relationship to that understanding what is communication? I begin the exploration of these issues in Chapter 7 by exploring the nature and theory of metaphorology exploring how humans "think" about anything. How does partial or indistinct experience result in recognition, assessment, and "decision" or *choice*? The proposition in the ensuing chapters relies on a theory of cognition and understanding based on metaphorology and George Lakoff's theories of conceptual metaphor.

To better appreciate the cognitive linguistic aspects of the human perception of order, it is first appropriate to further examine the field-effect of *choice* properties on the resonance between the collection of *choices* and the observer(s). The next chapter explores the interaction of *choice* properties as they converge in presenting an overall impression to the observer – an impression of vitality, of a system not only exhibiting *life* but also *thriving*.

References

1. Alexander, C, *The Nature of Order An Essay on the Art of Building and the Nature of the Universe: Book II - The Process of Creating Life*, Berkeley, CA: The Center for Environmental Structure, 2002, p 4.
2. Wirth N, "Program Development by Stepwise Refinement," *Communications of the ACM*, Vol. 14, No. 4, April 1971, pp 221–227.
3. Mills HD., "Top-Down Programming in Large Systems," in *Debugging Techniques in Large Systems*, R. Ruskin, ed., Prentice-Hall, Englewood Cliffs, NJ, 1971.

4. Parnas DL., "Designing Software for Ease of Extension and Contraction," *IEEE Transactions on Software Engineering*, Vol. 5, No. 2, March 1979, pp 128–138.
5. Boehm BW., "A Spiral Model of Software Development and Enhancement," TRW tech. report 21-371-85, 1985, TRW, Inc., I Space Park, Redondo Beach, CA 90278.
6. Brooks FP., "No Silver Bullet: Essence and Accidents of Software Engineering," *Computer*, Vol. 20, No. 4 (April 1987) pp 10–19.
7. Alexander C, *The Nature of Order An Essay on the Art of Building and the Nature of the Universe: Book II - The Process of Creating Life*, Berkeley, CA: The Center for Environmental Structure, 2002, p 84.

Chapter 6
A Vision of Thriving Systems

An information system (like any system) is an arrangement of interacting and interrelating components. I recount in Chapter 2 Alexander's revelation of the properties that express the quality of the interaction and interrelating occurring in a system of architectural components. This chapter explores the interaction and interrelating of the information system *choice* properties mapped to Alexander's *center* properties. I investigate the *choice* property interrelationships themselves and characterize the fundamental interaction as quality features that bespeak of great design in what I propose to call a *thriving system*.

6.1 The "Field-Effect" of Choice Properties

Wholeness (as Alexander describes it) is a "field" of interrelationships among *centers* in a "space" where the interaction of the *centers* resonates with the "self" of the "observer." Alexander puts it this way:

> The more carefully we think about each property and try to define it exactly, the more we find out that each property is partly defined in terms of the other fifteen properties. Although the fifteen properties seem distinct at first, they are in fact intertwined and interwoven. [1]

When these properties are mapped to *choice* properties, that "field" of interrelationships reveals the intensities as qualities that those *choices* of modeling and design reflect in the stakeholders' experience of the system. Design quality results from the strength of the interaction of all 15 *choice* properties as perceived in that *choice*. Properties individually may seem significant, others less so, and still others virtually absent in that *choice*. Individuals or groups of stakeholders are more or less sensitive to certain qualities. They experience them differently because of their perception of property intensities and the aspects of their particular concerns or investment in a system. However insensitive to an individual or subset of *choice* properties stakeholders may be, nonetheless it is the confluence of those property intensities that resonates with them

L.J. Waguespack, *Thriving Systems Theory and Metaphor-Driven Modeling*,
DOI 10.1007/978-1-84996-302-2_6, © Springer-Verlag London Limited 2010

in some manner to form their satisfaction with the system. Just as it is humanly impossible to observe the intensity of any one of Alexander's 15 *center* properties in the absence of any others, it is likewise impossible to experience a design *choice* as solely qualified by a single *choice* property.

Each *choice* property (as each *center* property) is experienced in a confluence of all 15. And although some may appear to predominate in that mix, none can be meaningfully isolated from the rest without diminishing the experience. This is both the mystery of art and the majesty of human perception and understanding. As Chapter 7 will explore, human perception and understanding achieve an enormous feat of recognition, pattern recognition, and classification that allows such a confluence of qualities to be experienced and assessed in composite, as a whole. And the satisfaction that is experienced (and sought) in design is a resonance of "self" with that whole conveying to the observer a sense of the *wholeness* of the system, a sense of order that is to each stakeholder – natural. Through the analysis of property interactions that follows, I will parse the field-effect of properties and associate property interactions with stakeholder-perceived design qualities. Some of these qualities are familiar to systems developers while others offer a new lens through which to assess design quality.

6.2   Choice Property Coherence

In Chapter 3, Table 3.1 depicts Alexander's insight into the interrelationships of the *center* properties by identifying which of the 15 properties are "supported" by which others. A "supporting" property is depended on or necessary for the understanding of the property it supports [1, p. 238]. His matrix not only gives insight into the meaning of each property (and contributes to the rationale for mapping them to *choice* properties), but also provides a means of grouping or clustering the properties by way of their supporting properties, and clustering the *choice* properties as well. To that end, I propose a measure of the affinity between *choice* properties based on the coincidence of their supporting properties. I call this measure *coherence* (see Table 6.1).

Coherence is calculated between two properties as the sum of the overlap of their supporting properties – their interrelationship or influence on one another. The overlap of property A over property B is determined by the fraction of B's supporting properties that are found among A's supporting properties. If half of B's supporting properties are found in A's supporting properties, then the overlap of A over B is 0.5. The overlap in the opposite direction determines the overlap of B over A. The sum of the two overlaps yields a number between 0 and 2. A value of 2 indicates complete bilateral overlap while 0 would indicate none. Based on *coherence*, a "distance" separating the two properties results by subtracting each overlap sum from 2 (i.e., the value 0 indicates complete *coherence* or no "distance," while 2 indicates maximum "distance," independence). For example, each

Table 6.1 Distance measures between properties based on *coherence*

	1	2	3	4	5	6	7	8	9	10	11	12	13	14	15
1	0.00	–	–	–	–	–	–	–	–	–	–	–	–	–	–
2	1.58	0.00	–	–	–	–	–	–	–	–	–	–	–	–	–
3	1.17	0.67	0.00	–	–	–	–	–	–	–	–	–	–	–	–
4	0.75	1.33	1.00	0.00	–	–	–	–	–	–	–	–	–	–	–
5	0.50	1.13	1.13	1.13	0.00	–	–	–	–	–	–	–	–	–	–
6	1.25	1.71	1.13	0.83	1.25	0.00	–	–	–	–	–	–	–	–	–
7	1.50	1.17	1.58	1.17	0.88	1.25	0.00	–	–	–	–	–	–	–	–
8	1.58	1.00	1.33	1.00	1.42	1.42	1.17	0.00	–	–	–	–	–	–	–
9	1.58	1.00	1.33	1.00	1.42	1.13	1.17	1.33	0.00	–	–	–	–	–	–
10	1.21	1.07	1.07	1.07	0.66	1.20	1.21	0.76	1.69	0.00	–	–	–	–	–
11	1.17	1.33	1.33	0.67	1.42	0.54	1.58	1.33	1.00	1.38	0.00	–	–	–	–
12	1.58	1.00	1.33	1.33	0.83	1.13	1.58	1.33	1.33	0.76	1.00	0.00	–	–	–
13	1.17	1.33	1.33	1.33	0.83	1.13	0.75	1.33	1.33	1.07	1.33	1.33	0.00	–	–
14	1.55	0.90	1.63	1.27	1.03	1.35	1.55	1.27	1.27	0.97	1.27	0.90	1.63	0.00	–
15	1.61	1.38	1.38	1.38	1.20	0.93	1.21	1.38	0.45	1.71	1.07	1.38	1.07	1.66	0.00

property is completely coherent with itself, a "distance" value of 0 – no separation. Table 6.1 depicts the complete tabulation of paired property *coherence* measures as "distance." Note that there are no "distance" values of 2.0 (total independence)!

6.3 Choice Property Clustering

Using these measures as indications of *coherence* between properties, it is possible to develop groupings that indicate related properties that share supportive characteristics. The process of determining these groupings is cluster analysis [2–4]. The clustering technique in use here is hierarchical, agglomerative clustering where clusters are formed as pairs of nearest "proximity." Once formed, the cluster is treated as a single element in the determination of the next cluster in the successive construction of pairs until all individual elements are assimilated.

The criterion for grouping is a "distance" measure that in this case is the *coherence* measure. The result of this pairwise clustering is a tree-structure where adjacent leaves depict elements so "close" as to be paired. The result of the clustering is found in Fig. 6.1.

The tree may be partitioned by trimming off "clusters of leaves" by snipping the inner branches at some level from the root (at the far left). Snipping at every branch results in the 14 clusters as depicted in Fig. 6.2.

In the hierarchical, agglomerative clustering technique, there is no prescribed or definitively useful "snipping point." The clusters represent "prospectively

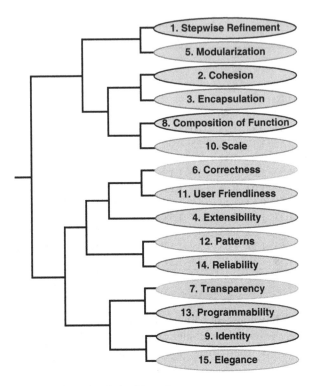

Fig. 6.1 *Choice* property clustering derived by *coherence*

useful groups" indicating the proximity or affinity of the member properties. Indeed at one extreme, the final clustering indicated by the root of the tree, "N," groups all the properties into a single cluster. The subdivision of this "super" cluster into constituent clusters offers the opportunity to explain the proximity, the affinity, the stakeholder-perceived quality of design *choices*, and exposes property patterns that contribute to the *wholeness* of a system design.

Clusters A--G are the finest granules of interdependency or property support. Observers, stakeholders, are more likely to recognize the effect of these clusters in the fine-grained *choices* they examine. Higher levels of agglomeration (i.e., clusters H, I, and J) reveal a greater confluence of effects as the combination of lower level clusters (in some sense more discrete) combine in a more complex convergence of effects. Clusters K, L, M, and finally N grow into the full confluence of all 15 *choice* properties. Each cluster is a framework for interpreting a palpable "field" of quality resonance in a design or modeling *choice* – simple or complex. I consider each cluster below in turn.

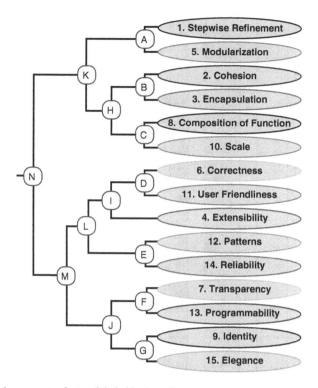

Fig. 6.2 *Choice* property clusters labeled by branch

6.4   Choice Property Cluster Contribution to Wholeness

Each of the clusters of *choice* properties represents a different emphasis or nuance of *living* structure features. At the same time, they remain interwoven in the field-effect of properties contributing in concert to the intensity of each *choice*. In the discussions of clusters that follow, the properties remain the same in whichever cluster they participate; however, their influence is nuanced by the confluence of all the properties in that cluster. As this review of clusters proceeds from those with the least number of properties per cluster to those with the greatest, the reader will note a growing degree of abstraction that describes the clusters' resonance as the weave of the interrelationships appears to shift the focus from the resonance of individual *choices* to the *wholeness* of an entire system.

Table 6.2 lists the 14 clusters determined by the branches of the clustering tree. It also lists the supporting properties of each property in the cluster. Properties found to support every property composing a cluster are noted in the darker shading. I refer to these as primary support properties. Primary support properties relate the effects of the cluster on observer perceptions to a greater degree than the rest of the supporting properties and provide a logical focus for explaining the cluster's character as a confluence in the cluster's field-effects.

Table 6.2 Property clusters and supporting *choice* properties

Cluster		Property Tree Cut at Branches																														
	14 Clusters	Row Item Supported by Column	1	•••	2	•••	3	•••	4	•••	5	•••	6	•••	7	•••	8	•••	9	•••	10	•••	11	•••	12	•••	13	•••	14	•••	15
A	1	Stepwise Refinement	1		2		3						6						9													15
	5	Modularization	1		2		3						6		7				9				11				13		14		15
B	2	Cohesion							4						7				9		10						13				15
	3	Encapsulation			2				4						7		8		9		10				12						15
C	8	Composition of Function							4		5						8		9				11		12						15
	10	Scale	1		2										7				9				11		12						15
D	6	Correctness	1		2						5		6				8				10				12				14		
	11	User Friendliness			2						5		6		7						10								14		15
E	12	Patterns	1										6		7						10		11		12		13				15
	14	Reliability	1										6		7				9				11		12		13				15
F	7	Transparency	1								5								9								13				
	13	Programmability	1				3				5				7				9										14		

G

#	Property	1	2	3	4	5	6	7	8	9	10	11	12	13	14	15
9	Identity			3		5			8	9	10			13		15
15	Elegance			3		5			8	9	10	11		13	14	15

H

#	Property	1	2	3	4	5	6	7	8	9	10	11	12	13	14	15
2	Cohesion				4			7		9	10			13		15
3	Encapsulation		2		4			7	8	9	10					
8	Composition of Function				4	5			8	9			12			15
10	Scale	1	2					7		9		11	12			15

I

#	Property	1	2	3	4	5	6	7	8	9	10	11	12	13	14	15
4	Extensibility		2			5	6		8	9						15
6	Correctness	1	2			5	6		8		10		12		14	15
11	User Friendliness		2			5	6		8		10				14	15

J

#	Property	1	2	3	4	5	6	7	8	9	10	11	12	13	14	15
7	Transparency	1				5				9				13		15
9	Identity			3		5			8	9	10			13		15
13	Programmability	1		3		5		7	8	9				13	14	15
15	Elegance			3		5			8	9	10			13	14	15

K

#	Property	1	2	3	4	5	6	7	8	9	10	11	12	13	14	15
1	Stepwise Refinement		2	3			6			9				13		15
2	Cohesion				4			7		9	10			13		15
3	Encapsulation		2		4			7	8	9	10					
5	Modularization	1	2	3			6	7		9		11		13		15
8	Composition of Function				4	5			8	9			12			15
10	Scale	1	2					7		9		11	12			15

(continued)

Table 6.2 (continued)

	Property Tree Cut at Branches	1	...	2	...	3	...	4	...	5	...	6	...	7	...	8	...	9	...	10	...	11	...	12	...	13	...	14	...	15
Cluster	14 Clusters																													
	Row Item Supported by Column																													
L																														
4	Extensibility			2						5		6				8		9												15
6	Correctness	1		2						5		6				8				10				12				14		15
11	User Friendliness			2						5		6								10								14		15
12	Patterns	1												7						10		11								15
14	Reliability											6		7										12		13				15
M																														
4	Extensibility			2						5		6				8		9												15
6	Correctness	1		2						5		6				8				10				12				14		
7	Transparency	1								5								9								13				
9	Identity					3				5						8				10						13				15
11	User Friendliness			2						5		6								10								14		15
12	Patterns	1										6		7						10		11								15
13	Programmability	1				3								7				9								13		14		
14	Reliability											6		7		8								12		13				15
15	Elegance					3				5						8				10		11						14		

N		1	2	3	4	5	6	7	8	9	10	11	12	13	14	15
1	Stepwise Refinement									9						
2	Cohesion				4			7		9	10			13		15
3	Encapsulation		2		4			7	8	9	10					
4	Extensibility		2	3		5	6	7	8	9		11		13		15
5	Modularization	1	2	3		5	6		8	9	10		12		14	
6	Correctness	1	2			5	6			9				13		
7	Transparency	1			4	5			8	9		11	12			15
8	Composition of Function			3					8	9	10			13		15
9	Identity	1	2				6	7		9		11	12			15
10	Scale		2			5	6				10	11			14	15
11	User Friendliness	1		3			6	7		9	10	11				15
12	Patterns	1				5		7						13	14	
13	Programmability			3				7	8		10	11	12	13		15
14	Reliability			3		5										

6.5 Exploring the "Field-Effect" of the Clusters

I explore each of the clusters produced from cluster analysis based on the *coherence* measure relating *choice* properties. Each section includes a figure depicting the cluster with its members and primary support properties. In addition, an accompanying table recounts a thumbnail description of each property involved in the cluster as a reader's reference. Finally, each cluster is "named" as shorthand to characterize the overall quality resonance affected by the cluster. Some of these names may be familiar to systems developers, but the reader should be careful not to assume a particular interpretation independent of the specific *choice* property interactions described herein.[1]

6.5.1 Divisibility: The Field-Effect of Cluster "A"

Cluster "A" is composed of *stepwise refinement* and *modularization* supported by *cohesion, encapsulation, correctness,* and *identity* (Fig. 6.3). The table that follows (Table 6.3) recalls the thumbnail description of each property member of the cluster and the properties found to support every member of the cluster.

In life, the construction and maintenance of every element in nature involves the presence of parts. The presence of these parts or modules is essential to the distribution of responsibility and the tolerance of complexity, both in evolution and survival. In human cognition, problem-solving is universally predicated on the ability to decompose situations to analyze and understand the whole as a system of parts, *choices*. Therefore, *modularization* is essential to structure both in construction and comprehension.

> divisible |di'vizəbəl|
> adjective
> capable of being divided *without a remainder.*

(*Definitions noted in this section are derived from the New Oxford American Dictionary*) [5].

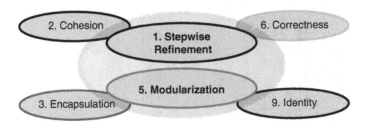

Fig. 6.3 *Divisibility* – Cluster "A"

---

[1]In preparing this text a wide variety of sources were searched to find "commonly accepted" definitions for the several familiar terms used to name the clusters. Surprisingly there was little definitive agreement among the sources. The reader may find that the specific characterizations of these terms may challenge some preconceptions. This may be particularly true with the scope of the meanings presented here.

Table 6.3 *Divisibility* cluster with supporting property descriptions

Cluster	Thumbnail property descriptions
A	**#1** *Stepwise refinement* reveals itself in a system when components scale up or scale down to reflect divide and conquer analysis and design allowing an observer to "zoom in" and "zoom out" and still retain a useful perspective effectively representing the system's primary concerns.
	#5 *Modularization*: A system is appropriately modularized when its subsystems are crafted to always work in combination with other subsystems to achieve their collective purpose for which individually they may be ignorant; reflecting a separation of concerns.
	#2 *Cohesion*: System components are cohesive when the well-defined design choices they embody reinforce their contribution to the system as a whole; the concerns central to each component are clear and distinct from the components that surround it.
	#3 *Encapsulation*: A system module is properly encapsulated when its separateness is balanced by a straightforward and intelligible description of "what" (defined by its interface) that module does to cooperate with the collective around it.
	#6 *Correctness* is the presence of germane and essential system behaviors as specified by the requirements combined with the absence of extraneous behaviors.
	#9 *Identity* is the clarity of distinctiveness between modules in a system, which prevents system components from addressing the same purpose and causing confusion within the design of the system as a whole.

Parts in and of themselves are not necessarily valuable. In fact, commonly in everyday life, parts exist as things that are broken, usually taken to mean no longer useful or usable. No longer existing as it was in the whole of its parts, it no longer retains the *identity* that it once was as the whole. Parts therefore may or may not be beneficial.

Beneficial parts emerge from a process that does not fracture the order that allows those parts to coexist (and cooperate) in a whole. *Stepwise refinement* reflects a goal-directed process of dividing a whole into parts that leaves the *identity* of the whole intact – disassembled but not destroyed. The process leaves the impression that the resulting parts still reflect the whole. The directing goal may be to derive divisions that reflect stakeholder familiarity, regulatory or professional standards, partitions for which known "solutions" exist or any number of strategies aimed at some form of effectiveness or efficiency. In any case, the goal is to render in parts and not diminish the *essence* of the whole; what it was or what the stakeholders perceived it to be still exists. For these reasons, *divisibility* is an apt name for the resonant quality, the field-effect of this cluster grouping *stepwise refinement* and *modularization*.

6.5.2   Factorability: The Field-Effect of Cluster "B"

Cluster "B" is composed of *cohesion* and *encapsulation* supported by *extensibility, transparency, identity,* and *scale* (Fig. 6.4).

The following table (Table 6.4) recalls the thumbnail description of each property member of the cluster and the properties found to support every member of the cluster.

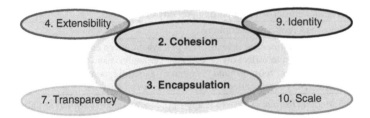

Fig. 6.4 *Factorability –* Cluster "B"

Table 6.4 *Factorability* cluster with supporting property descriptions

Cluster	Thumbnail property descriptions
B	#2 *Cohesion*: System components are cohesive when the well-defined design choices they embody reinforce their contribution to the system as a whole; the concerns central to each component are clear and distinct from the components that surround it.
	#3 *Encapsulation*: A system module is properly encapsulated when its separateness is balanced by a straightforward and intelligible description of "what" (defined by its interface) that module does to cooperate with the collective around it.
	#4 *Extensibility*: Modules that are conceived to be reused and retasked after they have been implemented are said to be extensible offering the potential for the system's function to be expanded even after the modules have been crafted.
	#7 *Transparency* is being able to observe discernible structure in a system; how things fit and work together and exposing the "patterns" and "weave" of their interconnectedness.
	#9 *Identity* is the clarity of distinctiveness between modules in a system, which prevents system components from addressing the same purpose and causing confusion within the design of the system as a whole.
	#10 *Scale* is the elaboration of system detail appropriate to the needs of particular observers used in complexity management in analysis, in design, in implementation, and in documentation.

Cohesion reflects the self-sufficiency of a *choice*; a *choice* that is well formed and thus is justified in its existence independent of the collection of *choices* around it. As small or as large a part of the domain it may be, each *choice* represents a stable, explicable, recognizable, namable granule of the whole.

---
factorize |ˈfaktəˌrīz|
verb [trans.] Mathematics
express (a number or expression) as a product of factors.

While *cohesion* faces inward, *encapsulation* turns outward. The clustering of *cohesion* with *encapsulation* accentuates the *choice*'s boundaries while providing a contractual interface through which it interacts and participates in the collection of *choices* around it. The protection implied through *encapsulation* insulates the *choice*'s inner details and promotes its stability while at the same time providing a published means of consistent collaboration with its surrounding *choices*. This combination of property effects denotes the *choice*'s role as a stable, credible part in the *wholeness* of the system – a contributing factor. For these reasons, *factorability* is an apt name for the resonant quality, the field-effect of this cluster grouping *cohesion* and *encapsulation*.

6.5.3 Constructibility: The "Field-Effect" of Cluster "C"

Cluster "C" is composed of *composition of function* and *scale* supported by *identity, user friendliness, patterns,* and *elegance* (Fig. 6.5).

The following table (Table 6.5) recalls the thumbnail description of each property member of the cluster and the properties found to support every member of the cluster.

Scale has the effect of focusing attention on a particular level of detail, rendering aspects at that granularity clear and discernible. *Composition of function* has the effect of constructing assemblies of progressive size and complexity by combining *choices* and combinations of *choices*. Once combined, these assemblies effectively fuse forming a new *choice* at a new level of *scale*.

---

construct

verb |kənˈstrəkt| [trans.]

• form (an idea or theory) by bringing together various conceptual elements, typically over a period of time.

The opportunity for combination of *choices* into more complex *choices* relies on the clarity of purpose and functionality that preexists in each constituent *choice*. The combining process usually follows a strategy or predefined pattern of assembly that permits expansion in both cardinality and complexity. When the "pieces" come together seamlessly or at least can be observed without undue regard for the "pieces" as "pieces," the overall impression is one of simplicity that reduces the barriers to usefulness and effective application. The expression of this quality in *choices* encourages stakeholders to consider adding capacity and function first by seeking out combinations of the existing *choices* rather than creating new ones. For these reasons, *constructibility* is an apt name for the resonant quality, the field-effect of this cluster grouping *composition of function* and *scale*.

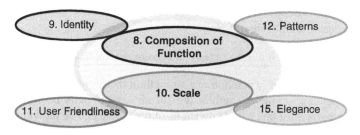

Fig. 6.5 *Constructibility* – Cluster "C"

Table 6.5 *Constructibility* cluster with supporting property descriptions

Cluster	Thumbnail property descriptions
C	#8 *Composition of function* implements its required functionality by combining components that interoperate with superordinate components to support a combined purpose. They tend to recede into the "shadows" as they perform their role largely anonymously forming new choices of function or behavior.
	#10 *Scale* is the elaboration of system detail appropriate to the needs of particular observers used in complexity management in analysis, in design, in implementation, and in documentation.
	#9 *Identity* is the clarity of distinctiveness between modules in a system, which prevents system components from addressing the same purpose and causing confusion within the design of the system as a whole.
	#11 *User friendliness* is achieved when the system is matched to the expectations of its users; the range and granularity of interface options reflecting the nature of the needs of the users in accomplishing their individual tasks.
	#12 *Patterns* in a system expose symmetry of purpose; similarities and parallels are reflected explicitly often described in standards, guidelines, and frameworks.
	#15 *Elegance*: System models that are consistent, clear, concise, coherent, cogent, and transparently correct exude elegance.

6.5.4 Confidence: The "Field-Effect" of Cluster "D"

Cluster "D" is composed of *correctness* and *user friendliness* supported by *cohesion, modularization,* and *correctness* (Fig. 6.6).

The following table (Table 6.6) recalls the thumbnail description of each property member of the cluster and the properties found to support every member of the cluster.

Correctness is the proper alignment of *choice* with stakeholder intentions. In that sense, there is no "absolute" *correctness* independent of stakeholder intentions. *Correctness* is a "moving target"; when intentions change, alignment must be adjusted. *Correctness* may be the first and most critical property of all. If stakeholder intentions cannot be expressed with *choice*(s) exhibiting strong *correctness*, the rest of the properties have no chance of delivering satisfaction. This is underscored by the fact that *correctness* is a supporting property of *correctness* (the only property so reflexive!). *Correctness* is at least transitive if not cumulative in its effects.

confidence |ˈkänfədəns; -fəˌdens|
noun
the feeling or belief that one can rely on someone or something; firm trust .

As in the *composition of function*, the strength of the *correctness* property of the whole is dependent on the strength of the *correctness* property of the constituent parts. Those parts must be credible divisions of the whole and be individually credible. *Correctness* and *user friendliness* reinforce each other as the alignment of the *choice* with the stakeholder intentions coincides with the user's expectations and

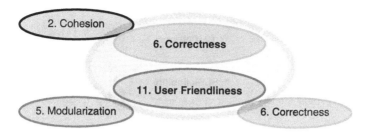

Fig. 6.6 *Confidence* – Cluster "D"

Table 6.6 *Confidence* cluster with supporting property descriptions

Cluster	Thumbnail property descriptions
D	#6 *Correctness* is the presence of germane and essential system behaviors as specified by the requirements combined with the absence of extraneous behaviors.
	#11 *User friendliness* is achieved when the system is matched to the expectations of its users; the range and granularity of interface options reflecting the nature of the needs of the users in accomplishing their individual tasks.
	#2 *Cohesion*: System components are cohesive when the well-defined design choices they embody reinforce their contribution to the system as a whole; the concerns central to each component are clear and distinct from the components that surround it.
	#5 *Modularization*: A system is appropriately modularized when its subsystems are crafted to always work in combination with other subsystems to achieve their collective purpose for which individually they may be ignorant; reflecting a separation of concerns.
	#6 *Correctness* is the presence of germane and essential system behaviors as specified by the requirements combined with the absence of extraneous behaviors.

their very perception of "what is natural!" Being able to "see" what you expect to find in a *choice* is vital to maintaining reliance and trust. For these reasons, *confidence* is an apt name for the resonant quality, the field-effect of this cluster grouping *correctness,* and *user friendliness.*

6.5.5   Predictability: The "Field-Effect" of Cluster "E"

Cluster "E" is composed of *patterns* and *reliability* supported by *correctness, transparency,* and *elegance* (Fig. 6.7).

The following table (Table 6.7) recalls the thumbnail description of each property member of the cluster and the properties found to support every member of the cluster.

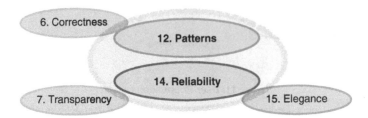

Fig. 6.7 *Predictability* – Cluster "E"

Table 6.7 *Predictability* cluster with supporting property descriptions

Cluster	Thumbnail property descriptions
E	#12 *Patterns* in a system expose symmetry of purpose; similarities and parallels are reflected explicitly often described in standards, guidelines, and frameworks.
	#14 *Reliability*: Reliable systems function as designed without interruption eschewing extraneous detail, thus avoiding unwanted or unexpected side effects that lead to unwanted and unnecessary system maintenance.
	#6 *Correctness* is the presence of germane and essential system behaviors as specified by the requirements combined with the absence of extraneous behaviors.
	#7 *Transparency* is being able to observe discernible structure in a system; how things fit and work together and exposing the "patterns" and "weave" of their interconnectedness.
	#15 *Elegance*: System models that are consistent, clear, concise, coherent, cogent, and transparently correct exude elegance.

If a problem-solving approach succeeds repeatedly, that may be the simplest and clearest indication that the approach subsumes the problem's *essence*. To successfully apply the familiar to the unknown is very comforting (and satisfying). The accumulation of the "successful familiar," those tactics and strategies that lead to repeated success, is a sign of vitality. Successful systems are composed of successful *choices* that are born of the repeated application of proven *patterns* developed through experience. The success of matching pattern to problem depends on the detection of those aspects to which the pattern is applicable and to the naturalness that the alignment between pattern effects and problem issues reveals to the observer. In those instances where the alignment is "perfect," the use of the pattern embodies an elegant solution.

> predictable |pri'diktəbəl|
> adjective
> behaving or occurring in a way that is expected.

Devising and accumulating patterns that apply consistently and yield consistent successes embodies the property of *reliability*. The most common risk in reapplying solutions of experience to new situations is the unexpected side effect; the case where the pattern's applicability nearly, but incompletely, matches the situation at hand. The remedy involves standard assessments that predict (if not certify) that a pattern is applicable before it is used. These assessments can be gathered into norms or frameworks that predict side effects and thus permit wasted effort and *choice* rework to be minimized. *Choices* that are formed by a well-balanced presence of *patterns* and *reliability* promote *predictability* and eschew the unexpected and unwelcome surprises. For these reasons, *predictability* is an apt name for the resonant quality, the field-effect of this cluster grouping *patterns* and *reliability*.

6.5.6 Usability: The "Field-Effect" of Cluster "F"

Cluster "F" is composed of *transparency* and *programmability* supported by *stepwise refinement, modularization,* and *identity* (Fig. 6.8).

The following table (Table 6.8) recalls the thumbnail description of each property member of the cluster and the properties found to support every member of the cluster.

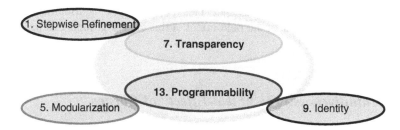

Fig. 6.8 *Usability* – Cluster "F"

Table 6.8 *Usability* cluster with supporting property descriptions

Cluster	Thumbnail property descriptions
F	#7 *Transparency* is being able to observe discernible structure in a system; how things fit and work together and exposing the "patterns" and "weave" of their interconnectedness.
	#13 *Programmability* provides users with the means to dynamically retarget the system over time; supporting a range of purpose achieved primarily by aggregating various collections rather than multiplying choices.
	#1 *Stepwise refinement* reveals itself in a system when components scale up or scale down to reflect divide and conquer analysis and design allowing an observer to "zoom in" and "zoom out" and still retain a useful perspective effectively representing the system's primary concerns.
	#5 *Modularization*: A system is appropriately modularized when its subsystems are crafted to always work in combination with other subsystems to achieve their collective purpose for which individually they may be ignorant; reflecting a separation of concerns.
	#9 *Identity* is the clarity of distinctiveness between modules in a system, which prevents system components from addressing the same purpose and causing confusion within the design of the system as a whole.

Except in the most abstract of circumstances, *choices* are subject to *accidents of implementation* where the "technology" used to represent the *choice* diverges from the mode of stakeholder expression. The closer the representation is to the stakeholders' conception of the *choice*, the greater the strength of the *transparency* property in that *choice*. When the intention of the *choice* is clear, it is easier for the stakeholder (user) to recognize and thus apply it to their task. On the contrary, a *choice* that obscures the intention is likely to be overlooked at best or misapplied at worst.

usable |'yo͞ozəbəl| (also **useable**)
adjective
able or fit to be used.

An important aspect of the applicability of a *choice* is the versatility that it offers. If its applicability is narrow and inflexible, the range of its use will also be narrow. If it is flexible, its range of use is likely to be broader and draw stakeholder (user) attention more readily and frequently. Frequent use results in familiarity, familiarity promotes a sense of naturalness, and that sense promotes reuse! The property of *programmability* is an expression of the versatility a *choice* provides through parameters, dialogs, inheritance, etc. For these reasons, *usability* is an apt name for the resonant quality, the field-effect of this cluster grouping *transparency* and *programmability*.

6.5.7   Intuitiveness: The "Field-Effect" of Cluster "G"

Cluster "G" is composed of *identity* and *elegance* supported by *encapsulation, modularization, composition of function, scale,* and *programmability* (Fig. 6.9).

The following table (Table 6.9) recalls the thumbnail description of each property member of the cluster and the properties found to support every member of the cluster.

Identity and *elegance* combine to characterize perceived naturalness. *Identity* fuses the conceptual with the linguistic when the name and the *choice* are indivisible

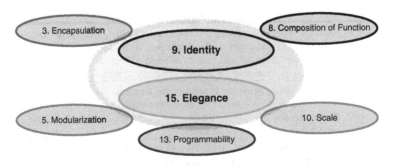

Fig. 6.9 *Intuitiveness* – Cluster "G"

Table 6.9 *Intuitiveness* cluster with supporting property descriptions

Cluster	Thumbnail property descriptions
G	#9 *Identity* is the clarity of distinctiveness between modules in a system, which prevents system components from addressing the same purpose and causing confusion within the design of the system as a whole.
	#15 *Elegance*: System models that are consistent, clear, concise, coherent, cogent, and transparently correct exude elegance.
	#3 *Encapsulation*: A system module is properly encapsulated when its separateness is balanced by a straightforward and intelligible description of "what" (defined by its interface) that module does to cooperate with the collective around it.
	#5 *Modularization*: A system is appropriately modularized when its subsystems are crafted to always work in combination with other subsystems to achieve their collective purpose for which individually they may be ignorant; reflecting a separation of concerns.
	#8 *Composition of function* implements its required functionality by combining components that interoperate with superordinate components to support a combined purpose. They tend to recede into the "shadows" as they perform their role largely anonymously forming new choices of function or behavior.
	#10 *Scale* is the elaboration of system detail appropriate to the needs of particular observers used in complexity management in analysis, in design, in implementation, and in documentation.
	#13 *Programmability* provides users with the means to dynamically retarget the system over time; supporting a range of purpose achieved primarily by aggregating various collections rather than multiplying choices.

in thought and expression. In the stakeholders' domain, it is usually assumed that names and concepts are perfectly aligned. Requirements engineers, however, are careful to test that alignment throughout the requirements analysis activity to detect conceptual "synonyms" and "homonyms" that are often unnoticed by the stakeholders themselves in complex environments. Strengthening *identity* results from properly bounding *choices* (*modularization*), protecting them from adulteration (*encapsulation*), matching them with complementary *choices* (*composition of function*), describing them in the proper context (*scale*), and defining an appropriate range for their applicability (*programmability*).

---

intuitive |in't(y)oōitiv|

adjective

using or based on what one feels to be true even without conscious reasoning; instinctive.

The field effect of *elegance* harmonizes a *choice*'s *identity* with the whole, balancing its impact and responsibility in the community of the whole. Its presence, its existence, its position in the whole are as if they could not have been conceived of differently; as if the *choice* as presented *is* the intention of the stakeholders. The strength of *elegance* is the resonance of the *choice*'s contribution to the *wholeness* of the system where the experience of the whole is greater than the sum of its parts. (In choral music, this phenomenon is expressed as the detection of an additional note in a chord as in hearing a fifth note in the chord sung by a barbershop quartet!)

For these reasons, *intuitiveness* is an apt name for the resonant quality, the field-effect of this cluster grouping *identity* and *elegance*.

6.5.8 Scalability: The "Field-Effect" of Cluster "H"

Cluster "H" is composed of *cohesion, encapsulation, composition of function,* and *scale* supported by *identity* (Fig. 6.10).

The following table (Table 6.10) recalls the thumbnail description of each property member of the cluster and the properties found to support every member of the cluster.

This cluster combines the properties that compose *constructibility* with those of *factorability*. Where *factorability* reflects a soundness of individual choices for their

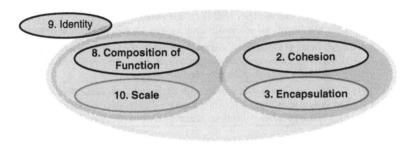

Fig. 6.10 *Scalability* – Cluster "H"

Table 6.10 *Scalability* cluster with supporting property descriptions

Cluster	Thumbnail property descriptions
H	#2 *Cohesion*: System components are cohesive when the well-defined design choices they embody reinforce their contribution to the system as a whole; the concerns central to each component are clear and distinct from the components that surround it.
	#3 *Encapsulation*: A system module is properly encapsulated when its separateness is balanced by a straightforward and intelligible description of "what" (defined by its interface) that module does to cooperate with the collective around it.
	#8 *Composition of function* implements its required functionality by combining components that interoperate with super-ordinate components to support a combined purpose. They tend to recede into the "shadows" as they perform their role largely anonymously forming new choices of function or behavior.
	#10 *Scale* is the elaboration of system detail appropriate to the needs of particular observers used in complexity management in analysis, in design, in implementation, and in documentation.
	#9 *Identity* is the clarity of distinctiveness between modules in a system, which prevents system components from addressing the same purpose and causing confusion within the design of the system as a whole.

internal stability and structural independence, *constructibility* reflects the capacity for joining *choices* in combinations that permit the building of larger and more complex arrangements.

scalable |'skāləbəl|
adjective
able to be changed in size or scale.

Interchangeability in connection, if not in function, is critical to the stability of structures. The opportunity to arrange by mixing and matching provides the range of options from which to choose the most appropriate (e.g., effective, efficient, economical, etc.). Component-based architectures are the "poster-child" of this quality where the product is composed of parts with the potential of many different combinations with a minimum of cost for rearranging them to achieve gains in capacity or complexity. For these reasons, *scalability* is an apt name for the resonant quality, the field-effect of this cluster grouping *cohesion, encapsulation, composition of function,* and *scale.*

6.5.9   Fidelity: The "Field-Effect" of Cluster "I"

Cluster "I" is composed of *correctness, user friendliness,* and *extensibility* supported by *cohesion, modularization,* and *correctness* (Fig. 6.11).

The following table (Table 6.11) recalls the thumbnail description of each property member of the cluster and the properties found to support every member of the cluster.

For whatever reason, *extensibility* did not participate in any of the binary property clusters.[2] Its affinity did not outweigh that of any of the other pairings. Combined with the cluster *confidence,* its importance to stakeholders is pronounced. Where *confidence* relates to a strength of reliance on *what is,* the addition of

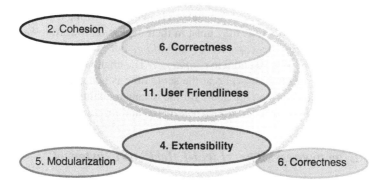

Fig. 6.11 *Fidelity* – Cluster "I"

---

[2]Since the clustering algorithm performs pair-wise aggregation the odd number of properties necessarily left an "odd man out!"

Table 6.11 *Fidelity* cluster with supporting property descriptions

Cluster	Thumbnail property descriptions
I	#4 *Extensibility*: Modules that are conceived to be reused and retasked after they have been implemented are said to be extensible offering the potential for the system's function to be expanded even after the modules have been crafted.
	#6 *Correctness* is the presence of germane and essential system behaviors as specified by the requirements combined with the absence of extraneous behaviors.
	#11 *User friendliness* is achieved when the system is matched to the expectations of its users; the range and granularity of interface options reflecting the nature of the needs of the users in accomplishing their individual tasks.
	#2 *Cohesion*: System components are cohesive when the well-defined design choices they embody reinforce their contribution to the system as a whole; the concerns central to each component are clear and distinct from the components that surround it.
	#5 *Modularization*: A system is appropriately modularized when its subsystems are crafted to always work in combination with other subsystems to achieve their collective purpose for which individually they may be ignorant; reflecting a separation of concerns.
	#6 *Correctness* is the presence of germane and essential system behaviors as specified by the requirements combined with the absence of extraneous behaviors.

extensibility shifts the effect from the present to the evolving incorporation of *what will be* the changing nature of both stakeholder intentions and the system's response to the changes in and among *choices*.

> fidelity |fə'delətē|
> noun
> faithfulness to a cause, demonstrated by continuing loyalty and support.

Accommodating the future, the inevitable change that it brings, influences the nature and *essence* of *choices* as they must in their aspiration toward *cohesion* and *correctness* account for the capacity of *unfolding*, but without sacrificing the strength of those properties essential to *confidence*. The challenge is building something that is correct in the now while at the same time is adaptable for the future. For these reasons, *fidelity* is an apt name for the resonant quality, the field-effect of this cluster grouping *correctness*, *user friendliness*, and *extensibility*.

6.5.10 Effectiveness: The "Field-Effect" of Cluster "J"

Cluster "J" is composed of *transparency*, *identity*, *programmability*, and *elegance* supported by *modularization* (Fig. 6.12).

The following table (Table 6.12) recalls the thumbnail description of each property member of the cluster and the properties found to support every member of the cluster.

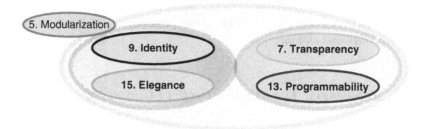

Fig. 6.12 *Effectiveness* – Cluster "J"

Table 6.12 *Effectiveness* cluster with supporting property descriptions

Cluster	Thumbnail property descriptions
J	#7 *Transparency* is being able to observe discernible structure in a system; how things fit and work together and exposing the "patterns" and "weave" of their interconnectedness.
	#9 *Identity* is the clarity of distinctiveness between modules in a system, which prevents system components from addressing the same purpose and causing confusion within the design of the system as a whole.
	#13 *Programmability* provides users with the means to dynamically retarget the system over time; supporting a range of purpose achieved primarily by aggregating various collections rather than multiplying choices.
	#15 *Elegance*: System models that are consistent, clear, concise, coherent, cogent, and transparently correct exude elegance.
	#5 *Modularization*: A system is appropriately modularized when its subsystems are crafted to always work in combination with other subsystems to achieve their collective purpose for which individually they may be ignorant; reflecting a separation of concerns.

This cluster combines the clusters of *intuitiveness* and *usability*. *Intuitiveness* reflects the naturalness the stakeholders' perceive in a *choice*: *what it is about* and how it "instinctively" addresses the intention for which it exists. It is the union of understanding the problem with understanding the solution.

> effective |i'fektiv|
> adjective
> successful in producing a desired or intended result.

Usability reflects the ease with which the stakeholder (user) can grasp and apply the *choice* to their purpose. This is promoted by both the clarity with which the *choice*'s intention is expressed (*transparency*) and with the versatility the *choice* offers (*programmability*) in adapting its use to a less than perfectly matched application. *Intuitiveness* reflects the *choice*'s impression as both native to the stakeholders' experience (*identity*) and natural in its representation (*elegance*). Stakeholders perceive *choices* possessing strong *intuitiveness* and strong *usability* to be "a natural *choice*!" For these reasons, *effectiveness* is an apt name for the resonant quality, the field-effect of this cluster grouping *transparency*, *identity*, *programmability,* and *elegance*.

6.5.11   Robustness: The "Field-Effect" of Cluster "K"

Cluster "K" is composed of *stepwise refinement, cohesion, encapsulation, modularization, composition of function,* and *scale* supported by *identity* (Fig. 6.13).

The following table (Table 6.13) recalls the thumbnail description of each property member of the cluster and the properties found to support every member of the cluster.

This cluster combines the clusters of *divisibility* and *scalability*. This cluster is all about sound static structure: the building blocks, their juxtaposition, their connectivity, their individual purposes, and how they all "hang together." *Divisibility* reflects the iterative decomposition that separates concerns among the *choices* and hones the representation of the *essence* that each embodies individually and (eventually) in composition. *Scalability* acts as the dual of *divisibility* by enabling the composition of *choices* carefully fusing their independent self-sufficiency into assemblies that can expand to meet the breadth and width of stakeholder intentions in a structure rigid enough to survive, yet pliable enough not to fracture.

robust |rōˈbəst; ˈrōˌbəst|
adjective
(of an object) sturdy in construction.
(of a process or <u>system</u>) able to withstand or overcome adverse conditions.

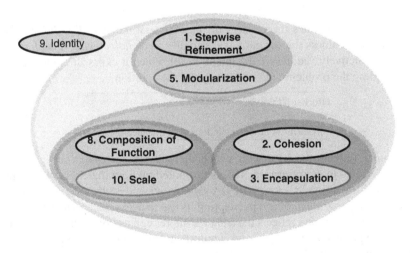

Fig. 6.13 *Robustness* – Cluster "K"

Table 6.13 *Robustness* cluster with supporting property descriptions

Cluster	Thumbnail property descriptions
K	#1 *Stepwise refinement* reveals itself in a system when components scale up or scale down to reflect divide and conquer analysis and design allowing an observer to "zoom in" and "zoom out" and still retain a useful perspective effectively representing the system's primary concerns.
	#2 *Cohesion*: System components are cohesive when the well-defined design choices they embody reinforce their contribution to the system as a whole; the concerns central to each component are clear and distinct from the components that surround it.
	#3 *Encapsulation*: A system module is properly encapsulated when its separateness is balanced by a straightforward and intelligible description of "what" (defined by its interface) that module does to cooperate with the collective around it.
	#5 *Modularization*: A system is appropriately modularized when its subsystems are crafted to always work in combination with other subsystems to achieve their collective purpose for which individually they may be ignorant; reflecting a separation of concerns.
	#8 *Composition of function* implements its required functionality by combining components that interoperate with superordinate components to support a combined purpose. They tend to recede into the "shadows" as they perform their role largely anonymously forming new choices of function or behavior.
	#10 *Scale* is the elaboration of system detail appropriate to the needs of particular observers used in complexity management in analysis, in design, in implementation, and in documentation.
	#9 *Identity* is the clarity of distinctiveness between modules in a system, which prevents system components from addressing the same purpose and causing confusion within the design of the system as a whole.

The resulting combination of qualities reflects structural integrity, a dependable foundation on which to grow an *unfolding* system. For these reasons, *robustness* is an apt name for the resonant quality, the field-effect of this cluster grouping *stepwise refinement, cohesion, encapsulation, modularization, composition of function,* and *scale.*

6.5.12 Sustainability: The "Field-Effect" of Cluster "L"

Cluster "L" is composed of *extensibility, correctness, user friendliness, patterns,* and *reliability* supported by *correctness* (Fig. 6.14).

The following table (Table 6.14) recalls the thumbnail description of each property member of the cluster and the properties found to support every member of the cluster.

This cluster is composed of *fidelity* and *predictability*. *Predictability* reflects maintaining a continuous, discernible trajectory of evolution while *fidelity* reflects the anchoring of *choices* in stakeholder intentions. In combination, they address the ecology of the system *unfolding*. As challenging as it may be to align a system of *choices* to the stakeholders' current understanding of reality, the prospect of anticipating how and in which direction that will evolve is even more so. Incorporating

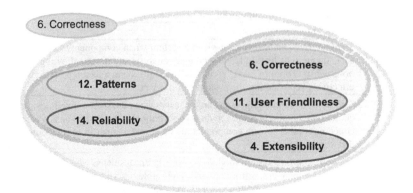

Fig. 6.14 *Sustainability* – Cluster "L"

Table 6.14 *Sustainability* cluster with supporting property descriptions

Cluster	Thumbnail property descriptions
L	#4 *Extensibility*: Modules that are conceived to be reused and retasked after they have been implemented are said to be extensible offering the potential for the system's function to be expanded even after the modules have been crafted.
	#6 *Correctness* is the presence of germane and essential system behaviors as specified by the requirements combined with the absence of extraneous behaviors.
	#11 *User friendliness* is achieved when the system is matched to the expectations of its users; the range and granularity of interface options reflecting the nature of the needs of the users in accomplishing their individual tasks.
	#12 *Patterns* in a system expose symmetry of purpose; similarities and parallels are reflected explicitly often described in standards, guidelines, and frameworks.
	#14 *Reliability*: Reliable systems function as designed without interruption eschewing extraneous detail, thus avoiding unwanted or unexpected side effects that lead to unwanted and unnecessary system maintenance.
	#6 *Correctness* is the presence of germane and essential system behaviors as specified by the requirements combined with the absence of extraneous behaviors.

that anticipation in the formation and combination of *choices* is what this cluster of qualities is all about. Long-term viability depends on the capacity to grow, to adapt, to evolve, to *unfold* toward the future.

sustainable |sə'stānəbəl|
adjective
able to be maintained at a certain rate or level.conserving an ecological balance.

Fidelity and *predictability* combine to express the quality of continuous movement coupled with continuous vigilance, guarding against changes that might allow the *essence* represented in system *choices* to drift apart from the evolving reality that stakeholders experience around them. For these reasons, *sustainability* is an apt name for the resonant quality, the field-effect of this cluster grouping *extensibility, correctness, user friendliness, patterns,* and *reliability.*

6.5.13 Vitality: The "Field-Effect" of Cluster "M"

Cluster "M" is composed of *extensibility, correctness, transparency, identity, user friendliness, patterns, programmability, reliability,* and *elegance* (Fig. 6.15).

The following table (Table 6.15) recalls the thumbnail description of each property member of the cluster.

This cluster is composed of *effectiveness* and *sustainability. Effectiveness* reflects the system's capacity to both effectively represent intentions as well as provide a collection of *choices* that are both understandable and applicable by stakeholders. *Sustainability* reflects the *unfolding* nature of the system where the collection of *choices* not only aligns with the current stakeholder reality, but is poised to respond to changes in shifting stakeholder intentions. The system expresses not only a relevant existence in the present, but also the capacity to grow and evolve with the stakeholder intentions into the future.

---

vital |ˈvītl|
adjective
indispensable to the continuance of life.
full of energy; lively.

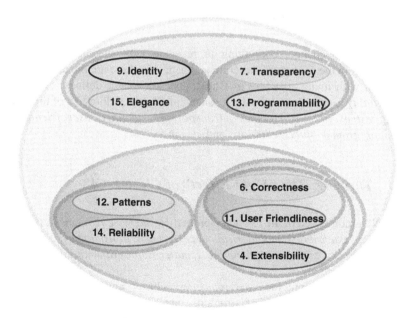

Fig. 6.15 *Vitality* – Cluster "M"

Table 6.15 *Vitality* cluster with supporting property descriptions

Cluster	Thumbnail property descriptions
M	#4 *Extensibility*: Modules that are conceived to be reused and retasked after they have been implemented are said to be extensible offering the potential for the system's function to be expanded even after the modules have been crafted.
	#6 *Correctness* is the presence of germane and essential system behaviors as specified by the requirements combined with the absence of extraneous behaviors.
	#7 *Transparency* is being able to observe discernible structure in a system; how things fit and work together and exposing the "patterns" and "weave" of their interconnectedness.
	#9 *Identity* is the clarity of distinctiveness between modules in a system, which prevents system components from addressing the same purpose and causing confusion within the design of the system as a whole.
	#11 *User friendliness* is achieved when the system is matched to the expectations of its users; the range and granularity of interface options reflecting the nature of the needs of the users in accomplishing their individual tasks.
	#12 *Patterns* in a system expose symmetry of purpose; similarities and parallels are reflected explicitly often described in standards, guidelines, and frameworks.
	#13 *Programmability* provides users with the means to dynamically retarget the system over time; supporting a range of purpose achieved primarily by aggregating various collections rather than multiplying choices.
	#14 *Reliability*: Reliable systems function as designed without interruption eschewing extraneous detail, thus avoiding unwanted or unexpected side effects that lead to unwanted and unnecessary system maintenance.
	#15 *Elegance*: System models that are consistent, clear, concise, coherent, cogent, and transparently correct exude elegance.

Responding to change, continuing to resonate with stakeholder intentions, *unfolding* both in the *essence* of structure and behavior, these are the underpinnings of a system with *living structure* as Christopher Alexander defines it. For these reasons, *vitality* is an apt name for the resonant quality, the field-effect of this cluster grouping *extensibility, correctness, transparency, identity, user friendliness, patterns, programmability, reliability,* and *elegance*.

6.5.14   Thriving: The "Field-Effect" of Cluster "N"

Cluster "N" is composed of all 15 *choice* properties: *stepwise refinement, cohesion, encapsulation, extensibility, modularization, correctness, transparency, composition of function, identity, scale, user friendliness, patterns, programmability, reliability,* and *elegance* (Fig. 6.16).

The final cluster combines the *robustness* cluster and the *vitality* cluster. *Robustness* reflects soundness of structure, integrity of form, and capacity for survival. *Vitality* reflects alignment between *choices* and stakeholders' intentions with the capacity for growth and *unfolding* over time and change. Conjoined these

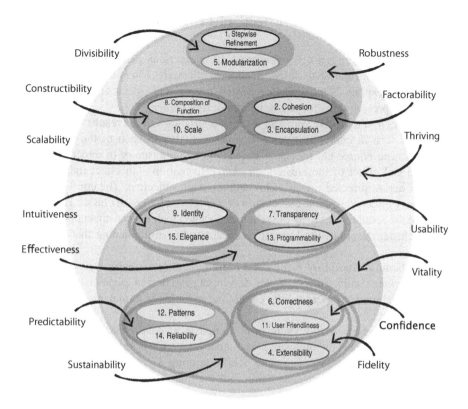

Fig. 6.16 *Thriving* – Cluster "N"

clusters express a quality beyond survival, beyond being alive. Robust, vital *choices* reflect a clarity of purpose, a dynamism, a vigor that emanates from the resonance between the stakeholders' intentions and the *choices* that represent them and (in most information systems) implement them.

> thrive |θrīv|
> verb
> grow or develop well or vigorously.
> • prosper; flourish

A system of *choices* strong in qualities of *robustness* and *vitality* is able to adapt (even predict) and thrive on change. It is able to grow on a path that aligns with the growth path of stakeholder requirements. The alignment reflects a symbiotic coexistence between what the system of *choices* achieves with what the system of *choices* is supposed to achieve according to the stakeholders.

For these reasons, *thriving* is an apt name for the resonant quality, the field-effect of this cluster grouping *stepwise refinement, cohesion, encapsulation, extensibility, modularization, correctness, transparency, composition of function, identity, scale, user friendliness, patterns, programmability, reliability,* and *elegance.*

6.6   Directing the "Field-Effect" of Property Clusters

The foregoing exploration of *choice* property interactions parses their individual and combined contribution to design quality. In effect, the 15 *choice* properties and the 14 clusters explain 29 hierarchically related, nondiscrete aspects of design quality. They lead to prescriptions for strengthening design *choices*.

In Chapter 4, a transitive verb and the characterization of the results of applying that action verb in *choice* formation was associated with each of the 15 *choice* properties. The *choice* clusters offer an analogous opportunity to understand the compositional effect of the clusters on *choice* formation – in effect indicating a course of action directed toward achieving a design objective. The confluence of the property effects defies the association of a single verb to each cluster. However, reviewing the results of applying the actions associated with the constituent properties of each cluster describes the formative objectives for strengthening that cluster's quality.

Strengthening *divisibility* results from strengthening *stepwise refinement* and *modularization* – which in turn means developing the design elements through an *unfolding*, elaborative process while employing modules as a fundamental element of construction.

Strengthening *factorability* results from strengthening *cohesion* and *encapsulation* – which in turn means distinguishing and separating each primitive element minimizing coupling between components while defining a contractual interface for each to hide/protect its implementation and facilitate its cooperation with other elements.

Strengthening *constructibility* results from strengthening *composition of function* and *scale* – which in turn means exploiting the opportunity to produce *choices* from the combination of existing *choices* that retain a relevance in the stakeholders' perception as deriving directly from their understanding of the *wholeness* of their intentions, a sense that the parts naturally subdivide and yet naturally recombine to meet their needs.

Strengthening *confidence* results from strengthening *correctness* and *user friendliness* – which in turn means aligning the *choice* in appropriate relationship to others and pursuing relevance, completeness, clarity, and conciseness in the rendered choice while accommodating the stakeholders' (users') sense of conformance with their belief of the *choice*'s purpose and function.

Strengthening *predictability* results from strengthening *patterns* and *reliability* – which in turn means discerning similarities among *choices* that may be repeated to promote the stakeholders' sense that an approach or feature is familiar and consistent, which further contributes to their sense of trust in the structure and function of the *choice* as "tried and true."

Strengthening *usability* results from strengthening *transparency* and *programmability* – which in turn means choosing *choice* features that expose rather than obscure the antecedent intentions so that system functions are "self-evident" in their role contributing to the users' problem-solving approach while providing a degree of flexibility such that the *choice* can be adapted to variations in the approach.

Strengthening *intuitiveness* results from strengthening *identity* and *elegance* – which in turn means unifying the *choice*'s representation with the intention it addresses such that the two fuse in the mind of the stakeholder. When this alignment between requirement and representation (implementation) occurs seamlessly, the naturalness of the fit gives the impression that the *choice is* the intention.

Strengthening *scalability* results from strengthening *constructibility* and *factorability* – which in turn means recognizing fundamental concepts that may be replicated and combined to render the stakeholders' conception of their intentions, and then by mapping those concepts to "building blocks" (*choices*) that may be combined and arranged to expand system size both in terms of capacity and complexity.

Strengthening *fidelity* results from strengthening *confidence* and *extensibility* – which in turn means achieving strong alignment of *choices* with stakeholder intentions now, but looking forward and preparing a structure and function of the *choice* that anticipates the inevitable realignment that must occur with the evolution of the context and priorities.

Strengthening *effectiveness* results from strengthening *intuitiveness* and *usability* – which means shaping *choices* that both take advantage of the stakeholders' instincts for problem-solving and further reinforce those instincts by presenting models with structure and functionality that mirror the stakeholders' perceptions of their needs.

Strengthening *robustness* results from strengthening *divisibility* and *scalability* – which in turn means successfully separating concerns among the *choices* clarifying the individual elements of *essence* that define the criteria of feasibility in the stakeholders' intentions while carefully formulating a resource of building blocks addressing those elements that may be combined and recombined to satisfy the need for capacity.

Strengthening *sustainability* results from strengthening *fidelity* and *predictability* – which means absorbing change gracefully without damaging the faithful alignment already attained between extant *choices* and stakeholder intentions.

Strengthening *vitality* results from strengthening *effectiveness* and *sustainability* – which means *choices* that satisfy stakeholder requirements and providing an accessibility to those *choices* that is understandable and obvious while maintaining an organization of structure and behavior responsive to an *unfolding* environment of stakeholder intentions.

When a system of *choices* exhibits strength across the confluence of design qualities described by *robustness* and *vitality*, it is a *thriving system – thriving* as in beyond existing, beyond surviving, beyond functional, beyond acceptable. It thrives because it *promotes* the *unfolding* not only of the *choices* that support and align with the stakeholders' intentions, but it actually *promotes* the unfolding of those intentions through the conceptual clarity and efficiency with which it represents them. *Thriving Systems Theory* represents the symbiosis that *great design* has with an authentic requirement. The challenge of great design spans two "fields" of perception: a design with strength in all the qualities enumerated above, but inexorably dependent on an authenticated representation of stakeholder intentions. Successful design must meet both "fields" of challenge.

6.7   The Consequence of Thriving Systems Theory

The 15 *choice* properties are interesting because they offer a taxonomy of observable characteristics that parse the resonance an observer experiences between any given *choice* and that which they conceive the *choice* should reflect. *Choice* properties provide two opportunities for understanding design quality: in assessing the existing *choices* and in forming (or reforming) new *choices*.

Indeed, several of the *choice* properties are commonly part of the systems architects' vocabulary: *modularization, cohesion, encapsulation,* and *composition of function*. At the same time, other *choice* properties are not so common: *correctness, user friendliness, patterns, reliability, identity,* and *elegance*. This apparent dichotomy is explained by the fact that systems architecture is more often focused almost exclusively on the soundness of product structure rather than on its faithful reflection of the stakeholder intentions. The named property clusters form an analogous dichotomy between sound structure and representation faithfulness, respectively: *divisibility, factorability, constructibility,* and *scalability* underlying *robustness* versus *confidence, predictability, usability, intuitiveness, fidelity, effectiveness,* and *sustainability* underlying *vitality* (see Fig. 6.17).

As separate as sound structure and representation faithfulness may appear, they interact just as the underlying properties interact. The quality of sound structure emerges from the building blocks that are designed to fit together in various ways giving flexibility and versatility to the built system. The economy of effort that the design of the blocks provides not only affects the costs (time, money, effort) of the build, but also affects the stakeholders' interpretation of their own intentions. When a structure *can* be built, it is natural to *want* to find a reason for building it.

That may explain the success of open source systems to some degree where the intentions of the consumers are in large part motivated by what the open source system is designed to do rather than being grounded first in their "preconceived" stakeholder intentions. In open source (Apache, MySQL, etc.) or proprietary vendor product situations (e.g., Oracle, Microsoft Office, Sun Java, etc.), it is as much the system design shaping the stakeholder intentions as anything else. "If you build it, they will come." Achieving structural and representational harmony is the interplay of both sides of the divide between built system (the side where the *choices* of the system are devised to satisfy the stakeholder requirements) and the other side, the side where the stakeholder intentions are conceived and expressed through requirements. The degree to which the "models" on either side of the divide reinforce one another and are compatible determines the success or failure of the resulting system, the degree of satisfaction that stakeholders experience.

The consequence of the coincidental, yet apparently dichotomous, presence of structural and representational design quality elements argues that great system design is not the perfect juxtaposition of elements in the product of a design process, but rather the effective juxtaposition of the *choices* in the design product with the *essence* found in the stakeholders' combined understanding of the requirements, their intentions. This latter relationship draws into aspect not only the effective reflection of the status quo, but a comprehensive understanding of the stakeholders'

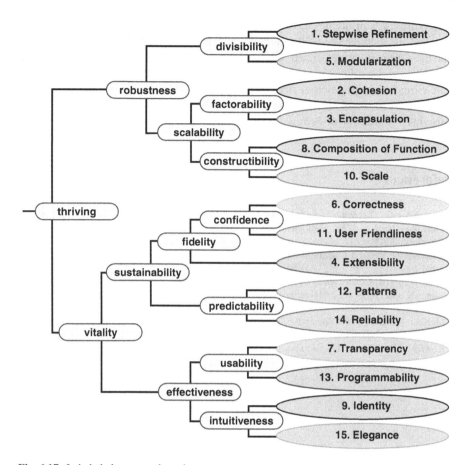

Fig. 6.17 Labeled cluster tree branches

environment, its ecology, and the prospects for the evolution of both. Exploring this consequence and the infusion of *Thriving Systems Theory* into systems development is the focus of part two of this monograph.

6.8 Historical Reverberations

Some 2,030 years ago, Vitruvius set down ten books defining the discipline of physical architecture as it was understood in the Roman universe [6]. As the only surviving treatise on architecture from those times, it provides a fascinating portal into the conceptualization of design in his lifetime. His treatise set forth three driving principles of valuable architecture: *firmitas* (strength), *utilitas* (functionality), and *venustas* (beauty). Although steeped in the culture and spirituality of that ancient time, Vitruvius's principles have echoed across the ages, as in DaVinci's Vitruvian Man and the architecture of the Renaissance, Baroque, and Neoclassicist periods. And those principles are echoed here in *choice* properties and property clusters. The *robustness* and *vitality* clusters derived in this chapter bear a striking congruence with Vitruvius's expression of *strength* and *functionality*. And when *robustness* and *vitality* are combined to form the cluster *thriving* – that composition embodies Vitruvius's expression of *beauty* (to be explored further in Chapter 11).

References

1. Alexander C, *The Nature of Order An Essay on the Art of Building and the Nature of the Universe: Book I - The Phenomenon of Life*, Berkeley, CA: The Center for Environmental Structure, 2002, p 237.
2. Aldenderfer MS and Blashfield RK, *Cluster Analysis*, Beverly Hills, CA: Sage Publications, 1984.
3. Anderberg MR, *Cluster Analysis for Applications*, New York: Academic Press, 1973.
4. Jain AK and Dubes RC, *Algorithms for Clustering Data*, Upper Saddle River, NJ: Prentice-Hall, 1988.
5. McKean E (editor), *The New Oxford American Dictionary*, Second Edition, 2051 p, May 2005, Oxford, UK: Oxford University Press.
6. Rowland D and Howe TN, *Vitruvius. Ten Books on Architecture*. Cambridge, UK: Cambridge University Press, 1999.

Part II
Thriving Systems Theory in Systems Development

The second part of the journey is applying the steps that progress toward your goal.

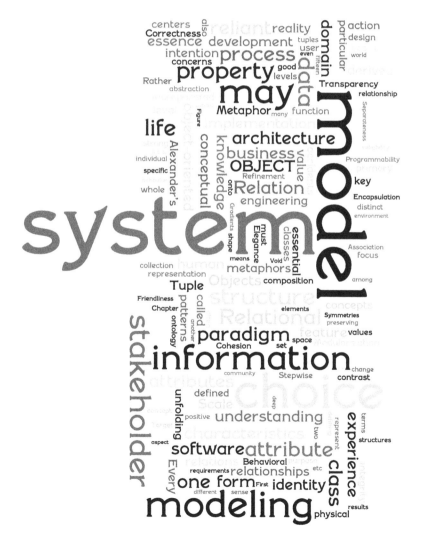

Chapter 7
Metaphorology

Metaphor is commonly associated with romantic poetry where the characteristics of one term are used to modify or restyle the intent of another. Used this way, metaphor serves a lexical function by intimating a meaning for which there is no specific word. In the last half century, science found that metaphor plays other key roles in communication and understanding. Research in metaphorology intersects neurology, psychology, philosophy, anthropology, archeology, and cognitive linguistics.

> [... M]etaphor is a very fundamental cognitive phenomenon: it lies at the basis of the structure of most abstract phenomena, such as abstract concepts, but also various types of cognitive models. In the 'Lakov-Johnsonian' view, metaphor receives a special position: it is no longer a phenomenon which is studied in the margin of certain disciplines, by scholars who are 'incidentally' interested in it. Rather, metaphor is shown to be an important and even essential aspect of human understanding, an aspect which must be taken into account in any theory of meaning (whether linguistic, philosophical, literary, anthropological, psychological, social or aesthetic.) [1]

The conclusions reported here rely primarily on results from George Lakoff et al.'s research findings in cognitive linguistics that explain various human behaviors relating to thought: learning, imagery, and abstraction. This discussion focuses on the role of conceptual metaphor in the recognition, retention, and processing of knowledge. Some might call this a study of "human understanding." The intent is to consider "How do humans understand systems?" and thus "How does that enlighten system modeling?"

7.1 The Basics of Conceptual Metaphor

A conceptual metaphor is a mapping or projection of the characteristics of one concept onto another for the purpose of explaining or casting the latter in terms of the former – "one kind of thing in terms of another" [2]. In contrast to poetic metaphor,

L.J. Waguespack, *Thriving Systems Theory and Metaphor-Driven Modeling*, DOI 10.1007/978-1-84996-302-2_7, © Springer-Verlag London Limited 2010

the purpose of a conceptual metaphor's "casting" of characteristics is not to "restyle" the meaning of the latter concept but rather to "impart meaning" to it.

> The two "things" which are united in a metaphor are no longer seen as lexical items but rather as concepts or gestalts, most often referred to as conceptual domains [...]. [3]

In cognitive linguistics, conceptual metaphor defines an understanding of one conceptual domain in terms of another; for example, using one person's experience of life to understand a different person's experience. A conceptual domain can be any coherently represented experience. Conceptual domains play one of the following two roles in conceptual metaphors:

(a) Source domain: the conceptual domain from which we draw metaphorical expressions
(b) Target domain: the conceptual domain that we try to understand or explain

Metaphorical expressions present themselves in the form of "TARGET is the SOURCE" where target is the concept to be characterized by the mapping of constituent elements from the source concept. That is to say that a target domain is to be understood in terms of a source domain (see Fig. 7.1).

Everyday human conversation is replete with metaphorical instances. In the following, TASK is the target and OBJECT is the source:

A TASK is an OBJECT TO BE LIFTED OR MOVED:

"I'm buried in paperwork this morning."

"I'm trying to get this off my plate."

"My work is piling up."

This last example also includes a second mapping:

QUANTITY is HEIGHT:

"Prices are rising out of sight."

"The gas gauge indicates we're low on fuel."

"I'm up to here with your complaints."

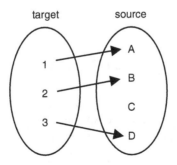

Fig. 7.1 Concept correspondence between source and target domains

In a metaphor, the correspondence of constituent elements characterizing the target in terms of the source is not usually one-to-one and onto, that is all the characteristics of the target domain are not determined by the source domain. However, the mapping of characteristics from source domain to target domain is usually *intentionally onto* – meaning that the features in the target domain intended to be characterized by elements in the source domain are all evident. (Note here that intentionally onto entails "aware" and "deliberate.") When the use of metaphors departs from this practice of *intentionally onto*, what often results is what are sometimes called mixed metaphors where the characterizations of the target are either contradictory or nonsensical.

A metaphor may exist as a self-contained mapping of understanding between domains. But metaphors commonly are found in collections that characterize a system of relationships and contributions more complicated than a single mapping. This collection phenomenon corresponds to that commonly found in cultural discourse.

LOVE is a JOURNEY:

"Our relationship has seen many <u>twists and turns</u>."

"We find our marriage <u>on the rocks</u>."

"Every love has to endure <u>bumps and potholes</u>."

"The <u>road is smoother</u> when two share the load."

"Counseling may be able to get us <u>back on track</u>."

7.2 The Metaphor in Thought: Lakoff's Embodied Mind

George Lakoff and Mark Johnson [2, 4] explain the nature and mechanisms of human understanding based on two premises. First, human cognition is based on categories, concepts, and experience. And second, cognition is based on primary metaphor arising from physical experience and subjective experience arising from extension and combination of primary concepts.

As physical beings, our awareness of the world is based on our sensorimotor experience of the world around us. We experience it through touch, taste, smell, sight (color), and sound. These experiences allow us to distinguish between event experiences (cold from hot, sweet from sour, fresh from rancid, light from dark, thunder from growl). Through continuous event experience and countless repetitions, we develop categories of experience that affect all forms of survival and satisfaction. The repetition and consistency of similar experiences give rise to a prototypical concept called a primary metaphor with which we identify the entire category.

Most of these categorizations become so ingrained as to be operable at a subconscious level. Human subjects can "sense" an understanding or recognition of concepts without the immediate capacity to explain it. The human brain possesses an experience processing facility attuned to the rhythms and structures of the natural environment – an environment richly populated by patterns that have survived the tests of eons. The physiology of the human brain is "hard-wired" to store, retrieve, and correlate memory aided by categorization. Concepts relating to survival and satisfaction are attributed to these primary metaphors and when a new event is categorized to a particular primary metaphor, its attributes are automatically ascribed to the new event (through immediate conceptual mapping via neural connections). Integrated in a spatial-motor sense of our surroundings (reaching for, moving toward or away from, being over, under, inside or outside of, surrounded by) the sensorimotor system of our experience is a continuous source of physical patterns to frame our consciousness and our subjectivity.

Life is a stream of primary metaphor experience that eventually yields patterns of these experiences that may be mapped to higher and higher levels of complex combination (conflation) in their relationship to survival and satisfaction. A combination of sights, smells, and sounds eventually becomes associated with (for example) food or mating. A different combination becomes associated with pain and thus danger or fear. The conflation of these patterns results in conceptual metaphors that overlap with a subset of the combined attributes of the constituent primary metaphors to which they relate. The subjective (e.g. striving for success, experiencing failure, making progress) is "felt" or realized in terms of a corresponding primary metaphor (i.e. searching for food, feeling injury, ascending the slope).

Human language provides ample evidence of conceptual metaphor's role in cognition. Magnitude is often expressed in terms of height, "The stock market is falling" or "The price of gas is sky high." Affection uses terms of distance, "We were close friends" or "We've drifted apart over the years." Control is explained as possession or containment, "You need to get a hold on yourself" or "I need to break loose of this crazy idea." Many of these metaphors are common to virtually every spoken tongue indicating that they are not simply idioms, but reflect an underlying conceptualization of magnitude, affection, or control. They reflect how the concepts are understood. And there are hundreds of other examples.

Lakoff's work also shows that metaphors are involved not only individually but also in collections that circumscribe concepts as in "Love is a journey," "Argument is a war," or "Research is a quest." As collections, the metaphors not only give language to concepts but they also give value and consistency to how a culture "thinks" about these concepts [2]. Lakoff et al. conclude that human thought, cognition, reasoning, and communication are based on a highly developed system of conceptual metaphors born out of our lowest level sensorimotor experience of the world. A system of conceptual metaphors may be localized to a community or culture, but many are virtually universal. A shared system of conceptual metaphors is fundamental to a community.

Not all concepts are metaphorical. All basic sensorimotor concepts are literal. Objects we experience directly (touch, taste, smell, see, or hear) are literal. Some subjective concepts are also literal. "This cup is the same color as that cup" is a literal concept. "This cup is nearly the same color as that cup" is a metaphorical concept using the metaphor of "distance" between the colors.

Human communication is heavily dependent on metaphorical "explanation." Literal concepts and primary metaphors combine in a structure of understanding organized around conceptual metaphor. Conceptual metaphors built up layer upon layer and relying on the underlying primary metaphors form an integral support for learning, recognition, and cognition – understanding. Lakoff and Núñez reaffirm these conclusions about human understanding explicating some of the most abstract forms of human reasoning – mathematics [5].

Adopting Lakoff's theory of human understanding, there is little difference (if any) in saying "system of conceptual metaphors" instead of "body of knowledge."

7.3 Lakoff's Embodied Mind Meets Alexander's Nature of Order

Lakoff's theory of the embodied mind exhibits an intriguing congruence with Alexander's theory of the nature of order, particularly Alexander's experiments with human subject perception of differing degrees of *life*. Lakoff's theory posits that a significant amount (perhaps the vast majority) of what cognitive psychologists consider "knowledge" resides in the human mind as a collection of conceptual metaphors that are built up and categorized over years of experience. This storehouse of "knowledge" is employed through the unconscious, reflex action of a pattern-matching brain that continuously searches for antecedent patterns of "experience" with which to make sense of the stimuli of the now. Some experiences match primary metaphors and categorize at the lowest level of conceptual complexity. Others require the conflation of two or more conceptual metaphors that provides an "explanation" of the experience by retrieving a categorical history from which they derive conclusions about the experience. Other experiences do not "make sense" until a new conceptual metaphor evolves through experience or until intentional, conscious learning, or conception constructs a new conceptual metaphor to ground the new experience in terms of prior existing "knowledge."

Alexander's theory would indicate that the consistent agreement of human subjects in the degree of *life* they perceive in architectural systems represents an innate concept of order. And since the overwhelming preponderance of agreement extends throughout and often beyond cultural boundaries, the concepts are truly "innate." This agrees with Lakoff's notion of the evolutionary synergy between the human brain and its environment. The patterns around us that persist reflect structures possessing an organization and behavior attuned to their natural environment enabling them to survive, even thrive; to be *living structures*. Those same *living structures* are the very key to the survival of the human organism sharing that environment. Through thousands of years of evolution, the human brain has developed aptitude in sensing, categorizing, and recognizing those *living structures* to satisfy the survival needs of its own host, the human being. And although observers may not be able to explain it, Alexander's research demonstrates that "they know it when they see it!"

7.4   Metaphors and Patterns

Structures consistent with characteristics of *living structure* lead to two important propositions for the modeling and the building process:

1. Structures possessing the properties of living structure should be more intuitively comprehensible to humans (modelers and observers).
2. Structures possessing the properties of living structure should be resistant to the systemic flaws that would injure their potential of operating in harmony with their environment. They should be inherently survivable.

In Alexander's books on architectural design, he proposed building patterns, "rules of thumb," for dealing with particular requirements arising in specific architectural design situations, metaphorical prescriptions in response to particular given characteristics [6, 7]. Those rules of thumb (253 in Alexander's pattern language book) amount to "good solutions by example." By directly following Alexander's footsteps, there was a flurry of work on pattern languages in programming (23 patterns in Gamma et al.'s book, some 150 in Coplien and Schmidt) [8–10]. Some 20 years after Alexander's pattern works, his treatise on The Nature of Order outlines his theory and principles founded on properties of *centers* that explain the morphogenesis of the pattern language work [11].

In Alexander's domain of physical architecture, the *unfolding* of structure is visible in the space, rooms, passage ways, courtyards, windows, byways, alleyways, neighborhoods, boulevards, etc. In the abstract domain of modeling and information systems, the *unfolding* structure is "visible" only in the portfolio of models and their features as they evolve toward the intended deployment. Observing the *unfolding* of the physical structures requires looking, walking over, and inspecting physical models. Observing the unfolding of the abstract structure of information systems is somewhat more difficult. The human mind needs a conceptual device with which to detail the *essence* of the model and expose the elements of *unfolding* as it occurs. The next chapter proposes that device for "observing" and "manipulating" the abstract structure, the conception of the system being modeled and the model itself as conjoined – modeling as the process of crafting conceptual metaphors.

References

1. Taverniers M, *Metaphors and Metaphorology: A Selective Genealogy of Philosophical and Linguistic Conceptions of Metaphor from Aristotle to the 1990s*, Academia Press, Gent, The Netherlands, 2002, p 119.
2. Lakoff G. and Johnson M, *Metaphors We Live By*, University of Chicago Press, Chicago, IL, 1980.
3. Taverniers M, *Metaphors and Metaphorology: A Selective Genealogy of Philosophical and Linguistic Conceptions of Metaphor from Aristotle to the 1990's*, Academia Press, Gent, The Netherlands, 2002.
4. Lakoff G. and Johnson M, *Philosophy in the Flesh*, Basic Books, New York, 1999.

5. Lakoff G. and Núñez R, *Where Mathematics Comes From: How the Embodied Mind Brings Mathematics into Being*, Basic Books, New York, 2000.

6. Alexander C, Ishikawa S, Silverstein M, Jacobson M, Fiksdahl-King I and Angel S, *A Pattern Language*, New York: Oxford University Press, 1977.

7. Alexander C, *A Timeless Way of Building*, New York: Oxford University Press, 1979.

8. Coad P, "Object-Oriented Patterns," *Communications of the ACM*, 35, 9 [September 1992]: 152–159.

9. Coplien J and Schmidt D, Eds., *Pattern Languages of Program Design*, Reading, MA: Addison-Wesley, 1995.

10. Gamma E, Helm R, Johnson R and Vlissides J, *Design Patterns: Elements of Reusable Object-Oriented Software*, Reading, MA: Addison-Wesley, 1995.

11. Alexander C, *The Nature of Order An Essay on the Art of Building and the Nature of the Universe: Book I - The Phenomenon of Life*, Berkeley, CA: The Center for Environmental Structure, 2002.

Chapter 8
Metaphor-Driven Modeling

As Lakoff and Johnson's research attests, conceptual metaphor represents a fundamental and natural organizing framework of human understanding. It seems efficacious to apply this framework's benefits to the task of representing and communicating knowledge about systems and modeling. It seems almost poetic to say "We need to understand a system as a model in terms of conceptual metaphor."

8.1 The Nature of Systems

The notion of "system" enjoys a plethora of discussion in the literature across many disciplines, but there is very little consensus on a widely applicable definition. This is because "systems" exist everywhere and the term is colored by the perspective of the observer! In the context of the discussion of systems in this monograph, let us posit the following set of propositions:

- A system is a subset of the universe, some reality.
- The art of system modeling is choosing a subset of the universe.
- The art of good system modeling is choosing an appropriate subset of the universe.
- Design is an alternative form of modeling.
- The art of design is accounting for everything in the subset.
- The art of good design is satisfactorily accounting for everything in the subset.
- The universe is composed of only two kinds of things: structure and behavior, both of which are dynamic (i.e. behavior changes structure and structure enables behavior).

Using the foregoing propositions, there are extant systems to understand, explain, or analyze. There are systems that we *will* construct and thereby (in a sense) will "expand" the universe as well. In the former, the task seems to be discovering what the "subset of the universe" is, and in the latter, it is constructing a new or revised "subset of the universe" that does not yet exist. Design is usually only considered relevant in the latter case. However, I assert that "design" is intrinsic to modeling in every case, and therefore, design is simply one form of modeling. The proposition that design quality and satisfaction are coupled resonates with Alexander's notion of the *life* in systems as in "fitness for purpose," it resonates with Brooks' as in "*essence* of fact," and it resonates with Lakoff's proposition that understanding/comprehension corresponds to a particular mechanism of abstraction: metaphor. In Lakoff's terms:

> ... [A]ny human knowledge of reality is necessarily *human*, i.e. it depends completely upon how *humans* **understand** reality. Humans can only see and make sense of reality by their position *within* it, they cannot have a "God's eye view of the world" [...] or "an external perspective that stands outside of reality [...]." The position of humans in the world means how they **experience** reality, how they interact with others and with the environment, or, in short, how they live. Since all experience is experienced individually, various understandings of reality emerge. Moreover, it is erroneous to think that our capacity to know reality is a result of the rational structure of the human mind, which is capable to *mirror* the pre-existing and eternal rational structure of reality. Instead, what plays a major role in our understanding of the world, is **imagination**, "our capacity to generate *novel order*," which includes our capacity to see "one kind of thing in terms of another thing," i.e. to "metaphorise." [1]

> We need to get comfortable with the idea that human beings are fundamentally *imaginative* creatures and that imaginative activity is occurring every moment of our lives in our perception, conceptualization and reasoning. [2]

A system, a reality, that is the target of our modeling is a confluence of stakeholder "experience" and "imagination." With this notion of system as a foundation, the sections that follow explore the range of modeling concerns affecting stakeholder satisfaction.

8.2   The Utility of Modeling

A model represents. A model takes the place of. A model is not the "real thing." A model is more convenient to manipulate than the "real thing." Inevitably, a model is always simpler than the "real thing" that it models. That is not to say that models are not complex. They may be, but they are always less complex than the "real thing" because modeling always omits some aspects of the reality. Those aspects explicitly chosen for depiction are often referred to as model "features"; they represent aspects that are noteworthy or important in the stakeholders' understanding of the system being modeled. Omitted aspects may involve magnitude or detail or context. In some cases, the omission may be offset by a substitution – sometimes a similar, but always a distinct characterization (interpretation) replaces some reality in the depiction. Were there no omissions or substitutions, there would be no advantage in employing the model in place of the "real thing!" The key to effective modeling is in the *choices* of what to omit and what to substitute in the depiction of the "real thing." The omissions and substitutions depend on two questions: "What do we want to know or learn about the 'real thing?' " and "What do we want to achieve in the model?"

In many cases, the "real thing" is already an abstraction, not a concrete, tangible artifact or organism, but an intellectual concoction conceived to achieve some goal, some understanding, or behavior. "Real thing" and "reality" are noted repeatedly here in quotation marks because with the possible exception of situations where there is only one stakeholder, the "thing" or "reality" being modeled is an amalgam of stakeholder perceived requirements. And as an amalgam, there really is no one "real thing" until a model exists in an attempt to define it. This is the case with information systems. Information systems are always almost entirely composed of abstraction – propositions of what depicts the shared or overlapping stakeholder perceptions. An information system may incorporate, represent, refer, or relate to concrete things (i.e. products, customers, shipments, buildings, organizations, etc.), but in itself it is an assemblage of abstraction. Modeling information systems involves manipulating abstractions of abstractions!

Models almost always exist in a hierarchy or a succession. Models depicting the most detailed, rudimentary knowledge or issues usually form the basis of the hierarchy. In a model of a concrete reality, the reality itself might be perceived as the "pedestal" on which all other layers of model would rest. Models of a more abstract focus on the "reality" (or of some other model) form "higher" layers or levels in the strata. Generally, the models farther removed from the basis express more generalities and less detail and usually characterize aspects more abstract than those nearer the basis.

Owing to the two motivating questions, "What do we want to know or learn about the 'thing?' " and "What do we want to achieve in the model?," each layer, each model, serves distinct purposes at that point in the hierarchy or succession. Depending on many factors (e.g. the complexity of issues, the mode of analysis, the technology of transformation, etc.) there may be any number of layers in a model hierarchy. The number of layers may be rather arbitrary often influenced by precedent, opportunity, or modeling technology. In some cases, such as among the business disciplines, certain strata routinely reflect characteristics that are of most interest to a particular segment of stakeholders. For example, it is common to find business models, business process models, enterprise models, information system models, and software models coexisting representing the same underlying enterprise. Each model represents those issues of most interest or relating to specific responsibilities of a particular subset of stakeholders. Each model depicts the same shared identity, but differs in what it omits and/or what it substitutes for the "reality" it depicts.

8.3   Modeling: Crafting Conceptual Metaphors

A model represents what is understood by means of projection. The modeler chooses model features to map onto "facts" and characteristics that stakeholders deem to be relevant. In most instances, the features are rendered by means of some form of abstraction substituting for and representing the stakeholders' requirements. The abstractions may incorporate scaling, symbolism, redaction, paraphrase, etc. Several models may coexist. Each results to some degree in a different set of features or representations reflecting the differing perspectives of a subset of stakeholders as to which relevant elements are required to satisfy their perceptions of "reality." This is the natural effect of stakeholder aspect where the concerns specific to each stakeholder influence the importance or unimportance of system characteristics. The quest is for a model in which each stakeholder can recognize a satisfying response to their individual requirements in the whole. The challenge is to design a conceptual metaphor, a model (or a set of congruous models), that at some level of abstraction satisfies the whole of the stakeholders' individually perceived requirements.

A model is a conceptual metaphor mapping modeling *choices* onto the "reality" formed by the compilation and integration of the stakeholder community's perceived requirements. The target domain is the "reality" being modeled while the model serves as the source domain.[1] In Lakoff's syntax, "The REALITY is the MODEL." The "reality" is characterized in terms of the model features, *choices* (see Fig. 8.1). In a *faithful model*, all the relevant stakeholder requirements would be characterized. "Faithful" means here "omitting no characterizations deemed essential by stakeholders." A faithful mapping from model features to stakeholder requirements is referred to as *intentionally onto*.

Several models may simultaneously achieve the quality of *intentionally onto* in their mappings, each representing a differing understanding of the underlying experience expressed as a set of features describing that experience from a particular stakeholder aspect. Multiple conceptual metaphors may coincide each forming a slice of abstraction highlighting distinct concerns in a model hierarchy.

Models are often crafted as cooperating collections of conceptual metaphors individually addressing particular characteristics while together forming a composite conceptual metaphor that addresses the system as a whole. This collection phenomenon corresponds to that commonly found in cultural discourse (e.g. "Love is a journey.").[2] The various individual metaphors often reflect the separation of concerns

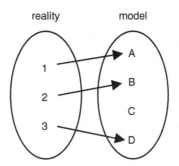

Fig. 8.1 REALITY is the MODEL

---

[1]See Section 7.1.
[2]See Section 7.2.

found in the system domain (e.g. in business: record keeping, contracts, inventory control, transaction review and approval, performance evaluation, forecasting, etc.). These individual metaphors may be organized around structural patterns that historically have served to explain (or define) a business practice or responsibility as in the designation of professional competencies (accountant, financier, marketeer, advertiser, or manager). They may be differentiated by the domain in which they are applied (retail, wholesale, government, services, research and development, construction, or manufacturing).

What about those features found in the model that do not map directly back to a "reality" characteristic? Can there be model features present for reasons other than *intentionally onto*?

8.4 Modeling Essence: Recognizing Accident

In the classic paper, "No Silver Bullet," Fred Brooks studies the problem of developing quality computer software [3]. He ascribes the problem's challenges to one of the two types of difficulty, essential or accidental. He attributes "essential" difficulties to the underlying problem to be "solved," independent of the development task at hand. This would be the "problem" as stipulated by the stakeholders and beyond the control of the developers. He attributes "accidental" difficulties not to the problem, but to the "means" developers choose to approach it – the development process, the development environment, the development tools, design patterns, the programming language, the computer configuration, etc. – any *choices* reached at the discretion of a developer. Therefore, Brooks' use of the term "accidental" is not in the sense of "happening by chance." He uses it as a philosophical term – "relating to or denoting properties that are not essential to a thing's nature," not *essential* to the purpose of the system.

Although Brooks' attention focuses on software development, his characterization applies equally well to the topic of modeling as discussed here. Those features mapped *intentionally onto* in a faithful model correspond to Brooks' essential difficulties. To omit any of the *intentionally onto* features would in effect be changing the problem, omitting some *essence*! Those features present for any other reason are accidental (as in *accidents of implementation*) because they are artifacts of the modeling activity rather than the system being modeled.[3]

Every system model is composed of some features that are *essential* representing defining aspects of the "reality" as the stakeholders see it. At the same time, because of the nature of modeling as a representation of "reality," every model also contains features that are *accidental* owing to the medium of expression (see Fig. 8.2). In the information systems domain, the media of expression may include

---

[3]See Section 5.5.

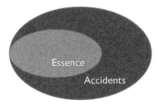

Fig. 8.2 Models composed of features: essential and accidental

mathematical formalisms, machine instruction sets, programming language dialects, graphical syntax, modeling paradigms, etc.[4]

Accidents of implementation are not extraneous to the development of quality computer software, but they are distinct from those elements satisfying the intention of the system's stakeholders. To operationalize the intention of the system, developers model the system function as computer function. Computer records implement social memory. Computer transactions implement social activities. Computer inputs, outputs, and interfaces implement social interactions. Each artifact entailed by the *implementation* of the intention, rather than the *definition* of the intention, is an *accident*.

Accidents of implementation are intrinsic to the extension of human intention in the system behavior through computerized realization as stored information (disks, tape, solid-state circuitry), programs (instructions, procedures), and processing (program execution, data transmission, computation, networking). Given any particular set of system characteristics, there are myriad technology options for the information system developer to consider in constructing the computer system. Countless options may be considered as prospective modeling choices. The deciding factor for any particular option could be economy (e.g. cost to build, cost of technology, cost to own), or expediency (e.g. compatibility with pre-existing resources, flexibility for expansion, reliability of suppliers, familiarity with the technology, etc.) – none of which are necessarily germane to the intention of the system. *Accidents of implementation* must exist – the critical concern is that they must be distinguished from *essence*!

Accidents of implementation can arise unexpectedly from apparently innocuous decisions in any modeling process. For example, in beginning the system modeling process, it is common to choose a "modeling tool"[5] that renders a drawn representation of the system. But, most such tools are intended to represent a finished system rather than a system "in utero." A modeler may at the outset wish to draft a "container" for information.

---

[4]In Alexander's domain of physical architecture the media of expression would be doorways, walkways, windows, terraces, beams, arches, paint colors, moldings, and any other artifacts of physical construction and design. In the domain of music the media of expression might be percussion, wind instruments, string instruments, key, pitch, melody, counterpoint, etc.

[5]Tool may be a graphical technology, an ontological vocabulary, or a computer assisted modeling tool as in C.A.S.E. tool.

The tool may allow the modeler to choose one of a predefined list of options (e.g. file, deque, queue, heap, array, list, etc.). Although the *choice* of container made at this time may indeed be the one that survives into the final rendering, at the outset of the process the *choice* is clearly arbitrary in the sense discussed above. And so, the representation medium for drafting the emerging model in itself potentially prejudices the process. This is just one of the hundreds of influences from which *accidents of implementation* can arise. To resist these influences, the modeler must adopt a system of thought, a mindset, that is keenly aware of the influences, but is not distracted by them – a mindset focused on intention.

So, how then can any means of specification or implementation be used and not contaminate the conceptual *unfolding* process? Again, it is not *what* the modeler uses, but *how* the mind is set in the process. The mindset must retain a constant focus on *essential* system characteristics. Identifying them and making *choices* that map with fidelity to the requirements is the most critical success factor. The modeler needs to be consistently mindful that the goal of the modeling process is to produce a conceptual metaphor that:

1. Results in a model feature set mapped *intentionally onto essential* system characteristics and
2. Explicitly designates any features included for *accidental* purposes

8.5   Quality Through Conceptual Metaphors

Model quality is the fusion of two interwoven sources of stakeholder satisfaction: (1) the degree to which a model's feature *choices* map *intentionally onto* the whole of the stakeholders' requirements and (2) the intensity with which the model *choices* exhibit the 15 *choice* properties.[6] Capitalizing on the first source of quality depends on the effectiveness of the modeling team (in union with the stakeholders) in challenging stakeholder perceptions of requirements as *essence* or *accident*. While *essence* must be guarded and preserved throughout the modeling and development process, *accident* represents an opportunity (responsibility) for crafting *choices* guided predominantly by the second source of model quality, the 15 *choice* properties. The 15 *choice* properties characterize order in the collection of *choices* – an order that promotes the stakeholders' intuitive understanding of the *choice*'s role and relationships in the collection and an order that contributes to the evolutionary survivability of the *choice* individually and in harmony with the whole.

Accidents of implementation should truly not be unfortunate incidents that happen unexpectedly and unintentionally. In the modelers' mindset, these should be opportunities for crafting a model that not only survives and has *life*, but indeed *thrives*. Maintaining a *life*-infusing mindset, focused on the goals above,

---

[6]See Section 3.16.

is a significant challenge particularly given the context of complexity and concerns that usually surround the modeling process. The next chapter examines that context and the challenges that threaten *life* in system models.

References

1. Taverniers M, *Metaphors and Metaphorology: A Selective Genealogy of Philosophical and Linguistic Conceptions of Metaphor from Aristotle to the 1990's*, Academia Press, Gent, The Netherlands 2002, p 136. *(original typography)*
2. Johnson M, *The Body in the Mind: The Bodily Basis of Meaning, Imagination and Reason*, University of Chicago Press, Chicago, IL, 1987, p 350.
3. Brooks FP, "No Silver Bullet: Essence and Accidents of Software Engineering," *Computer*, Vol. 20, No. 4 (April 1987) pp 10–19.

Chapter 9
Protecting *Life* in System Life Cycles

System development methodologies are variously devised to focus on and address specific development concerns. A project team chooses a methodology to shape what is known as an SDLC for the system under development. To some, SDLC reads "software development life cycle" while to others it reads "system development life cycle." The distinction may appear insignificant. The distinction may be critical, however, if it denotes a distinct difference in the scope of awareness for the *choices* that result.

In most cases, a development methodology and the SDLC it shapes are marked by a series of tasks that produce models evolving from generality reaching toward implementation specificity while at the same time shifting back and forth among modeling paradigms that emphasize one or another aspect of the target system. Modeling paradigms evolve to address clearly identifiable risks that recur in particular circumstances. They usually focus on specific concerns or problems in constructing a "useful" information system. The challenge in crafting a development methodology is to achieve an approach that addresses a fusion of concerns rather than creating a confusion of concerns.

Practically speaking, "information systems development" or "business application development" is a service activity. It is a service in the sense that these implements are constructed to serve a purpose outside of themselves, that of a business (organization, government, nonprofit, or community). The development process itself is usually so complex and expensive that the *purpose* focus of an information system development is sometimes underemphasized. Ideally, it would be nice to think of "the information system" as resolving a synthesis of concerns that span business purpose, user interaction, and beyond.

How does a focus on specific concerns integrate and contribute to the overall building of a *thriving* information system? Representing and preserving *essence* and recognizing artifacts of *accident* are critical to preserving *life* in the information system *life* cycle.

L.J. Waguespack, *Thriving Systems Theory and Metaphor-Driven Modeling*, DOI 10.1007/978-1-84996-302-2_9, © Springer-Verlag London Limited 2010

9.1   Common Models of System Concerns

As we have seen, the same system is often represented by several different models prepared to depict distinct mappings from the source domain of model features onto a target domain of stakeholder perceived system characteristics.[1] The different models place emphasis on different elements of concern. The variety may be due to distinct stakeholder perspectives, but is frequently due to distinct developer concerns.

Along with the *intentionally onto* features of each model, there may be a substantial accumulation of *accidental* features based on the concerns of developers rather than other stakeholders. The "same" system may be rendered in a cascade of models that focus on:

1. The defined/understood purpose, values, and objectives held by the business itself (a business model)
2. How the user understands it (a user requirements model)
3. What business activities occur in it (a business process model)
4. What information is collected, transformed, and reported by it (a data model)
5. The interactions the user has with it (a user interface model)
6. What the system does to "represent" the users' experience of interacting with it (an information/transaction model)
7. What decision and computing steps are taken by it using what information (a process model)
8. What computing infrastructure supports the "representation" of it (a hardware/ software configuration model), etc.

Development progresses through some subset and/or sequence of these models evolving toward an executable, deployable model. Each model may result in added *choices* that are *accidents of implementation*, to advance feasibility, economy, and/or convenience. What of the *essential*?

9.2   Model Conjugation and Transparency

Each model derived using a particular paradigm exposes specific concerns and offers particular devices for resolving them. Some paradigms attempt to be "all inclusive" in that they permit the depiction of any and all kinds of description about the target system as may be available. Other paradigms focus so completely on some issues that other issues are excluded to the point that there are no semantics with which to represent them in the paradigm. In this latter case, it is common that one system is depicted by more than one model at a time (e.g. in tandem) – each representing characteristics in its own special dialect. This might be likened to authoring the laws of a government where those relating to real estate are written

---

[1]See Section 8.3.

in Latin while those regarding traffic are set down in Greek, others in Chinese or in German, etc. The challenges of such an arrangement are obvious. It is not, however, uncommon to find several paradigms at work in a single SDLC. There are obvious benefits when a single paradigm suffices for the modeling required in a project. (This has been one of the major inducements for adopting the object-oriented paradigm, which will be employed to explore *life*-preserving structures in system development later in Chapter 12.) For the sake of clarity (sanity), the discussion in this chapter will continue considering systems modeled in only one paradigm at a time.

As the system characteristics are composed in one model representation and then another (as in the common models above), there is what the models hold in common (from one representation to the next) and what is distinct. If the models are to be recognizable as depicting the same system, there must be a common set of characteristics, a "signature," that is apparent from one model to the next. This is evident in the strength of the *choice* property called *transparency* and is a test of a "faithful" model that the "signature," the essential set of characteristics, remains traceable in the model. *Transparency* evidences the continuity of the *essence* from one model representation to the next in the *unfolding* system structure. To preserve *life*, essential characteristics must remain apparent every time their representation is transformed.

Model representations need to be transformed for many purposes. The list that follows generalizes the variety of transforms commonly found in information system modeling:

1. Explication – recasting or reorganizing the represented understanding from one model in the next model in terms convenient for a particular audience
2. Complexity Management – abstraction, partitioning, or simplification to reduce the number of concepts drawing attention – channeling attention to specific concerns
3. Conjugation – casting the antecedent model's characteristics in a form with desired syntactic or semantic formalism(s) for one of the following purposes:

    (a) Analysis – A modeling formalism suitable for logical or automated transformation or analysis: algebra, calculus, or set logic, etc. (e.g. to assess completeness or consistency)
    (b) Translation –
        • A diagramming discipline suitable for visual presentation: Entity Relationship, Unified Modeling Language, etc.
        • A machine translatable dialect: XML, SQL, Java, C++, etc., suitable for machine execution

If we think of a model as a repository holding facts/knowledge/understanding about the system being described, each of the transform varieties above presents opportunities for an increase or decrease in information content from one model representation to the next.

If the purpose in transforming a model is explication, one would normally not expect an increase or decrease in the information describing the system, but rather, simply a change in the presentation of that information for the purpose of making it accessible to a particular audience. An example might be translating a description written in English into another "natural" language such as French or Chinese. Although all such translations are imperfect (in an absolute sense), the difference in meaning is expected to be minimal and unintentional. (An exception here may arise when the target audience requires only a casual understanding of the system. The explication might take a form more akin to linguistic metaphors in which the system is described in terms of a generalization or a more familiar system with similar characteristics.)

In transforming a model to manage complexity facts/knowledge are sometimes purposefully omitted (abstraction, simplification, even redaction) to reduce the volume of information needed to convey some understanding. This occurs when the omitted information falls outside the interest of the audience and does not affect the purpose of the model from their perspective. In this case, strictly speaking, knowledge is lost. Only some subset of the system's signature is retained straddling the models. In contrast, reorganizing system knowledge (partitioning) does not omit but simply repackages system information in a form more convenient for the subsequent model's authors/users.

In transforming by conjugation, a whole range of fact/knowledge manipulation may occur. Modeling formalisms may add disambiguation details to the representation (which requires that more *essential* detail is sought and added to amplify the existing concepts). The knowledge is cast in some canonical form subject to proven manipulations in an algebra or calculus that transforms model information in a manner nondestructive and (usually) reversible. Rendering system descriptions in this form is often intended to offer interchangeability between modeling formalisms facilitating automatic or "machine-based" analysis.

Transformation accomplished through computing formalisms may result in computer-based simulation or "execution" of the model's intention. In this form of transformation, there are many representational constraints imposed by the computing formalism itself. Since transformation using these computing formalisms is often the last in a sequence of model representations, these representation *choices* are sometimes referred to as "implementation decisions." In fact, every representation dialect requires "implementation decisions" of one kind or another. The results of these decisions are what Fred Brooks called "accidental difficulties" [1] and what I call *accidents of implementation*. Mitigating *accidents of implementation* in these model transformations is the primary endeavor of software engineering research.

Accidents of implementation can be particularly insidious. The "side effects" of inattentively using any of these formalisms emerge not only in the effects on the clarity and ease of use of the resulting artifacts, but also may lead to "prejudice" in the antecedent model(s). Preconceptions may influence the characterization of system understanding, prejudicing the specification of the system's purpose. Presuming or anticipating which tool or formalism will be applied to a future transformation of a user requirement, a business process model, an interface model, or an algorithm often entices a modeler at that stage to cast interpretations onto the system that are not only superfluous, but sometimes obfuscate the real system intentions. The result becomes that *confusion* of concerns, an obstacle to system *life*, rather than the *fusion* of concerns that enables *life*.

9.3   The Paradox of Modeling Essence in the Now

This chapter began by asserting that the difference between interpreting SDLC as software development life cycle rather than system development life cycle may be critical. Clearly, overemphasizing the former by placing extreme focus on the computing implements of a systems development project to the neglect of the context of stakeholders and partners (both organizational and automated) leads inevitably to overlooked critical success factors. "Peripheral vision" is a must for keeping all the *essentials* in focus.

However, the objective of maintaining *transparency* in a series of system models presents somewhat of a paradox when one realizes that one edge of the periphery of context is the future. On the one hand, preoccupation with prospective paradigms or technologies may be detrimental to preserving a clear view of the *essence* of the system. At the same time, assessing probable, even plausible, channels of emerging requirements is critical to achieving the *transparency* of that *essence* and preserving *life* into the future. The paradox then is that achieving the "best" *choices* in the now depends on both developers and stakeholders being attentive to the future. "Best" will only be discernible in hindsight, which means that *choices* will need to be revisited, reevaluated, and later improved once they are informed by the future as it becomes the present.

How often *choices* need to be revisited depends on how long the "now" is. In domains such as telemarketing or internet commerce, where requirements change very quickly, the "now" may be weeks or months, while in other domains such as governmental regulation the "now" may be years. The duration of "now" itself becomes part of the *essence* of the system characteristics – as quality in the *choices* is affected by how flexible, adaptable, and responsive to change *choices* can and will be. It is in this regard that care in the modeling of *accidents of implementation* and the appropriate attention to *choice* property strength in that modeling can mean the difference between an arduous, expensive incorporation of changing system features versus a graceful *unfolding* in system evolution.

Reference

1. Brooks FP, "No Silver Bullet: Essence and Accidents of Software Engineering," *Computer*, Vol. 20, No. 4 (April 1987) pp 10–19.

Chapter 10
Metaphor-Driven Systems Engineering

Chapter 2 adopted a novel definition of information system as "an organized and integrated collection of *choices*." This terminology may be different from that commonly used in professional information system practice, but is it inconsistent? The synthesis of Alexander's vision of *living structure* and Lakoff's explanation of knowledge and understanding via metaphor provides an elegant framework for contemplating the effective design and construction of information systems as an organized and integrated collection of *choices*. The two prominent domains of professional IS practice that address the design and construction of effective information systems are software engineering and systems engineering. They share an underlying concept of patterning loosely defined in what are called software and/or systems "architecture." Although their perspectives are different, their underlying philosophy is the same and may be best explained through the unifying aspect of *choices*.

The synthesis of *wholeness* through *choices* and metaphor-driven modeling forms a vehicle for examining software and systems engineering principles and practices, both for the purpose of understanding them as well as exploiting their potential in information system development. The discussion that follows correlates the sense of importance of sound architecture that they share with the strength of *choices*, *wholeness*, and *life* in systems.

10.1 Software Engineering

"Software engineering is the application of a systematic, disciplined, quantifiable approach to the development, operation and maintenance of software" [1]. Software engineering was born of the realization that "software that runs" is not always a "problem solved." Software engineering broadens the focus on information system development beyond programming and computer hardware technology. It respects the building process while promoting a greater awareness of the context and motivations behind a system being built. However, software engineering's scope of concerns remains focused on the production of software artifacts and tends to be preoccupied with software and hardware technology to mechanize information system fabrication.

L.J. Waguespack, *Thriving Systems Theory and Metaphor-Driven Modeling*,
DOI 10.1007/978-1-84996-302-2_10, © Springer-Verlag London Limited 2010

10.2   Systems Engineering

The "engineering process" is also core to the practice of systems engineering.

> Systems engineering is an interdisciplinary approach and means for enabling the realization
> and deployment of successful systems. It can be viewed as the application of engineering
> techniques to the engineering of systems, as well as the application of a systems approach
> to engineering efforts. [2]

It is the "systems approach" that peaks the interest of the information systems development community. As an "interdisciplinary approach," systems engineering "casts a wide net" attempting to enlist the aid of perspectives that address human and societal influences on the effectiveness of systems. This facet is fully consistent with the *choices* characterization. At the same time, systems engineering brings a discipline of metrics to the process for estimating work, assessing progress, and identifying opportunities for process and product improvement. This is the "engineering process."

10.3   Ordering the Now/Accommodating the Future: Architecture

Both systems engineering and software engineering have a great interest in the concept called architecture. Both assert that a "sound architecture" is the key to effective and efficient systems. Ironically, neither discipline has succeeded in proffering a widely accepted definition of architecture. The Software Engineering Institute at Carnegie Mellon University solicits definitions for software architecture from practitioners and researchers worldwide. Their list currently exceeds 150 distinct definitions from more than 25 countries [3]. Perhaps, there are so many variations because systems and software architecture have lost their identification with Christopher Alexander's passion, physical architecture.

SEI and ANSI/IEEE variously define systems architecture as follows:

> System architecture is means for describing the elements and interactions of a complete
> system including its hardware elements and its software elements. [4]
> or
> The fundamental organization of a system, embodied in its components, their relationships to
> each other and the environment and the principles governing its design and evolution. [5]

Bass et al. define software architecture as:

> The software architecture of a program or computing system is the structure or structures
> of the system, which comprise software elements, the externally visible properties of those
> elements and the relationships among them. [6]

The state of software architecture as a topic of practice and research has been very active over the last two decades. Although some report that software architecture is well understood and has even reached a "golden age," [7] reports abound indicating there remains ample opportunity for improvements in the efficiency, economy, and effectiveness of computer-based information systems. Stakeholder satisfaction requires more than the latest innovations from hardware and software vendors and the gems of software engineering.

There is no question that inefficient software constrains the effectiveness of systems (and if software is inefficient to the extreme, it can contribute to system ineffectiveness). Attention to software architecture and the efficiencies it affords are necessary ingredients in efficient information systems – necessary, but not sufficient to make a system effective. Efficiency has no meaning in the absence of effectiveness. No degree of software efficiency can suffice in the absence of a faithful model of the system. Software engineering regularly fabricates finely machined software systems. However, it is the collection of *essential choices* that embody the goals and aspirations of a stakeholder community, which define system effectiveness, not the finely machined software system. Effectiveness arises not as the structure or configuration of software, but as the collection of *essential choices* that the software system "breathes into **life!**" In that regard, it is the architecture both in software and in systems that defines the framework of understanding that enables both efficiency and effectiveness.

10.4 Architecture in Thriving Systems Theory

The architecture of physical structures has been a topic of discussion and contemplation ever since humans began to shape their own environment, rather than simply accepting their surroundings as they found them [8]. The only truly consistent defining aspect of physical architecture is that groups of structures are recognizably related due to identifiable features or patterns of features. Recurring frequently enough, particular patterns are named and become associated with periods in history, geographical locales, or social groups because they exhibit recognizable similarities. The popularity of any particular named architectural style often accrues to the affects or impression that the style has on the inhabiting community. The effects may be security, comfort, inspiration, or perhaps nostalgia. In any case, designing or building based on an architectural style involves incorporating that recognizable pattern of features within the whole of the structure.

In *Thriving Systems Theory*, *architecture* is defined as a stable subset and pattern of *essential choices* (see Fig. 10.1). They are stable because they characterize articulation points and creases in the *unfolding* structure of the system (the model). Consider the paper folding analogy. A crease in a sheet of paper facilitates a fold or a bend, this way or that way along the crease while preserving the entire sheet as a whole and prescribing the potential folds that might predictably follow. It is not easy to fold or bend the sheet across or against the crease. If the paper is forced to bend in a way contrary to a crease, it will at least buckle, if not tear, thus defeating the *wholeness*, contradicting the folding intention of the crease. In the same way, articulation points prescribe options for the *unfolding* as a model or system evolves in the changing context of stakeholder perspectives and intentions. The options,

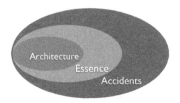

Fig. 10.1 The "Stable" or "Pattern" subset of essential features embodies the architecture

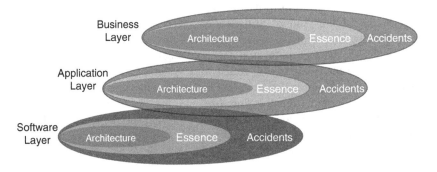

Fig. 10.2 Each layer or stratum of model may profess its own architecture

articulation points, predict the evolving structure, define the potential extensions, and constrain the future structure to a form that remains in harmony with its legacy [9]. Any collection of *choices* that evolves from these articulation points will be recognizable as having *unfolded* from them, and thus, the architecture's signature and *transparency* are preserved. An architecture engenders a "family" of offspring models or systems where each clearly reflects that certain parentage – that "architecture."

Because *architecture,* as defined here, characterizes *choices,* it is relative to the layer or level of abstraction that those *choices* entail. It is appropriate to speak of "software architecture," "application architecture," as well as "systems architecture," and even "business architecture" or "business process architecture" – each of which addresses a pattern of *choices* specific to that segment of stakeholder concerns (see Fig. 10.2). An *architecture*'s usefulness derives primarily from the stability that it facilitates in a layer of abstraction by anticipating *choices* specific to that segment of stakeholder concerns. A stable *architecture* is useful as it normalizes vocabulary, default functionality, and provides a foundation for discourse and negotiation among its stakeholders. Among the *choices* that are *essential* in modeling a system, those that are perceived to be most stable, remaining so through the foreseeable system evolution, form an *architecture*. These *choices* capture the least volatile definition and stakeholder understanding of the system's *identity*. And as a system may be a composition of several subsystems or subcomponents, each in turn may also have its own local *architecture*.

Following a particular *architecture* (somewhat like an ontology) shapes the stakeholders' expressive power in describing their intentions. Akin to the "chicken and the egg" paradox, it is not unusual for an *architecture* to be promulgated specifically to affect a stable pattern of *choices* that "pin down" some aspects of the moving target of stakeholder intentions – "Which comes first: the requirements or the architecture?"

Developers as one segment of stakeholders are very active in the formulation and promotion of *architectures* for any number of hardware and software domains: communications, instruction sets, protocols, data models, process models, user interfaces, graphics, photo imaging, video imaging, etc. Many of these *architectures,* through advocacy and negotiation, reach a level of formal recognition and are called standards.[1] They are all carefully formed collections of *choices* that address concerns at a specific level of abstraction in a modeling (and/or implementation) domain. Standards are sometimes incorporated as "construction sets" called frameworks that effectively represent prefabricated, partial modeling solutions. They are valuable tools when they are matched to a familiar, recurring problem, because they can limit the effort and expense that would be involved in creating an original solution from scratch. The care and precision involved in devising these *architectures* is an accurate archetype for the rigor involved in the formulation and specification of *choices* that result in a *thriving system* at any and each of the system, application, and business layers of modeling.[2]

10.5 Essence Versus Accident: Bifurcation or Continuum?

Effectiveness lies in the *essential* functionality deployed in a faithful model of the system, while efficiency lies in the judicious application of *accidents of implementation* that contribute to both system and software efficiency. *Essential choices* defining the "body of knowledge" ("system of conceptual metaphors") delineate the information and behavior that stakeholders stipulate as the "required system." This is the "essential structure" of the system that must be preserved, regardless of how it is modeled or brought to realization through engineering. Managing and maintaining the ongoing fidelity of the *essential choices* is the task of preventing or deterring *functional obsolescence*, while managing and maintaining the ongoing relevance of the *accidental choices* is the task of preventing or deferring *operational obsolescence*.

It would be most convenient if the distinction between system characteristics that constitute the *essence* and those that emerge as *accident* were always unambiguously divisible. The distinction, however, lies again in the perception and intention of the stakeholders. By the same result of stakeholder aspect that may

---

[1]Standards in one form or another are common to virtually all the professions to normalize terminology and practice to portray their behavior as predictable, orderly, and (to some degree) trustworthy.

[2]The cost associated with the rigor required cannot always be justified by the stakeholder community. The commitment to building a thriving system must be predicated on that community's cost/benefit assessment.

deem some characteristics as "unnecessary" and thus extraneous, some characteristics may not be seen as much as *defining* the system, but more like one of the several ways of *realizing* it. The designation of *essence* versus *accident* is a continuum rather than a bifurcation of features modeling a system.

Preserving *life* in the building of information systems starts long before computer technology becomes involved. It begins with the stakeholders' formulation of their intentions and the degree to which they can orient their perceptions in the system domain of legacy, environment, policy, implementation technology, usage, and the future (see Fig. 10.3).

The exchange of perspectives among the stakeholders and the negotiation required to reach any semblance of consensus deserve much attention prior to and throughout the entire lifespan of any system under consideration. Keeping all these perspectives refreshed and in view is the modeler's "peripheral vision" challenge.[3, 4] Those *choices* that are *essential* by definition or consensus and exhibit little likelihood for change over the foreseeable lifespan of the system are *prime* candidates for inclusion in the system's *architecture*. Those faculties of the system that

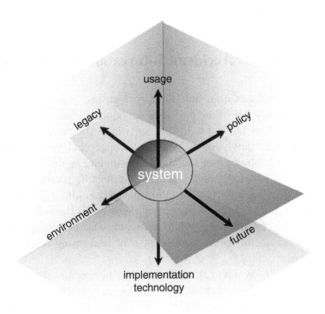

Fig. 10.3 The context of stakeholder perception and intention

---

[3]See Section 5.6.

[4]Aircraft pilots refer to this continuous peripheral scanning as situational awareness. Pilots must be ever attentive in a three-dimensional space. The stakeholder "space" may have several more dimensions in which they must be alert.

specifically accommodate or even facilitate an expected change would be *good* candidates for the system's *architecture*. *Choices* that reflect intentions expected to change are *poor* candidates for the system's *architecture*. Those *choices* solely selected for the "convenience" of the developers require designation as *accidents of implementation*. *Choices* that reflect the only single known means of realizing an essential aspect should also be designated as *accidents of implementation* because they must clearly be revisited as soon as alternative approaches become available. There is no "best" *choice* until there are alternatives from which to choose!

10.6 Information Systems Ecology: Managing Life

The key to understanding the *life* in information systems is to realize that at its core an information system is not "a" structure – it is an evolving organism. Unlike a software system where boundaries can be delineated and its static parts defined and cataloged, an information system is in continuous flux because of its social situation. *Architecture* is a key tool in managing the path of *life* for this organism. *Architecture* is not the structure of what has been constructed, as much as it is the template that enables, constrains, and fashions each evolving system instantiation. The challenge for systems architects is to identify the metaphors, the collection of *choices* that define the template, and then to form structures that are effectively malleable, disposed to metamorphosis, the *unfolding*. In this manner, an information system is not fabricated, it evolves through the collection of *choices* that the stakeholder community negotiates. Each new model or generation of model is a progression in the *unfolding*. The system architect's goal is to maintain the *unfolding* of system functionality without break or interruption in harmony with the environment, policies, usage, and implementation technologies, maintaining a seamless continuity with the legacy of stakeholder needs, while effectively anticipating the needs that can be expected in the future (see Fig. 10.3). This is the *life*-preserving process of transformation that Alexander describes for his buildings. A system (model) that *unfolds* in this process not only survives, but *thrives* as it not only absorbs inevitable change, but anticipates it and facilitates adaptation without surrendering the plasticity that future change requires.

   Perhaps, because of the massive effort required to bring even simple behaviors to realization in the early days of computer programming or because of the predominance of managers today immersed in the details of implementation technology or because the business stakeholders are intimidated by their information technology partners – for whatever reason, the definition and nurturing of the system-defining collection of *choices* and metaphors do not always receive the organizational care or priority required to promote a "healthy" information system ecology. Remarkably, each ecological failing can be traced either to a lack of or to the neglect of focus on the aspects of *essence* and *accident*; or on one or more of the 15 properties contributing to the strength of *choices* and *wholeness*. Each flawed decision, weak *choice*, contributes to a break or interruption in the *unfolding,* the evolving *life,* of the system. An uninterrupted progression of strong *choices* not only promotes *life* but a system that *thrives.*

Continuity, harmony, is achieved by following Alexander's "fundamental process" as follows: ("***choice***" substituted for "***center***" in the following)

1. *At each step, the process begins with a perception of the whole. At every step (whether it is conceiving, designing, making, maintaining or repairing) we start by looking at and thinking about the whole of that part of the world where we are working. We look at this whole, absorb it, try to feel its deep structure.*

2. *Within the whole, we consider the latent [choices] which might be worked on next. These latent [choices], are dimly, partially visible, large, medium and small.*

3. *We choose that one of these latent [choices] which, if established or strengthened next, will do the most to give the whole an increase of life. We work to intensify that living [choice], intensifying it in a way which, we judge, does the most good to the whole.*

4. *At the same time that we try to enhance the living quality of the chosen [choices], we also try to make it intensify the life of some larger [choice] that it belongs to.*

5. *Simultaneously, we also make or strengthen at least one [choice] of the same size as the [choice] we are working on and make it positive, next to the [choice] we are currently concentrating on.*

6. *Simultaneously, we also start to see and make and strengthen smaller [choices] within the one we are working on – increasing their life, too.*

7. *Once the whole has been modified by this operation, we start again* [10].

10.7   Checklist for Modeling Thriving Systems

The challenge for IS development is to wrap Alexander's "fundamental process" around the specific building goals and objectives using information technology to achieve the *life* that he seeks for physical architecture. A simple but effective first response to the challenge is incorporating the 15 *choice* properties into the modeling mindset. At each *choice,* a developer (architect, analyst, modeler, designer, programmer, administrator, stakeholder) has the opportunity to examine that *choice's* efficacy by applying the following checklist to assess the *choice's* contribution to the intensity or strength of the information system *wholeness.*

Does this *choice* contribute to the model's *wholeness* evidenced by the strength of:

1. *Stepwise Refinement?*
2. *Cohesion?*
3. *Encapsulation?*
4. *Extensibility?*
5. *Modularization?*
6. *Correctness?*
7. *Transparency?*
8. *Composition of Function?*
9. *Identity?*

10. *Scale?*
11. *User Friendliness?*
12. *Patterns?*
13. *Programmability?*
14. *Reliability?*
15. *Elegance?*
    and
16. Does this *choice* reflect *essential* characteristics of the system's purpose?
17. Does this *choice* represent an *accident of implementation* that should be documented as such for future reconsideration?
18. Does the model at this stage represent a recognizable, effective conceptual metaphor depicting the stakeholders' composite vision of the system ready for continued *unfolding* toward deployment?

The first 15 checklist elements directly follow from Alexander's properties of *centers* mapped to information system modeling *choices*. The next two are derived from the principles of Brooks' *essence* and *accident* applied to the metaphorical representation of human understanding. Emerging from Lakoff's theories of human understanding and cognition, the last checklist element acts to synthesize all the others by acknowledging that "time and *life* march on" and that *thriving systems* both absorb as well as anticipate the evolving environment of stakeholder intentions, upon which a system's quality is assessed. These questions form a *life-preserving mindset* centering on *wholeness* and dwelling on *choice* properties that infuse the system *life* characteristics that allow it to *thrive*.

This chapter began with an assertion,

> The synthesis of Alexander's vision of **living structure** and Lakoff's explanation of knowledge and understanding via metaphor provides an elegant framework for contemplating the effective design and construction of information systems as an organized and integrated collection of **choices**.

Efficient systems also require representation tools (paradigms, semantics, and syntax) that allow *essence* to be expressed and manipulated with a minimum of wasted mental energy. In this regard, software engineering strives consistently to improve the modeler's toolset. In Chapters 12 and 13 that follow, I explore the object-oriented and relational paradigms as mediums for achieving strong *choice* properties in *life-preserving* structures and transformations that yield *thriving* information systems. But before that – Chapter 11 considers whether there may be a more visceral sense of a *thriving system*, a sense of a system's beauty.

References

1. IEEE, "IEEE Standard Glossary of Software Engineering Terminology," IEEE std 610. 12-1990, 1990.
2. Thomé B, *Systems Engineering: Principles and Practice of Computer-based Systems Engineering*, Chichester, UK: Wiley, 1993.

3. SEI Community Software Architecture Definitions, http://www.sei.cmu.edu/architecture/start/community.cfm. Accessed 1/25/2010.
4. SEI Glossary, http://www.sei.cmu.edu/architecture/start/glossary/. Accessed 1/25/2010.
5. ANSI/IEEE 1471-2000, http://standards.ieee.org/reading/ieee/std_public/description/se/1471-2000_desc.html Accessed 1/25/2010.
6. Bass L, Clements P, and Kazman R *Software Architecture in Practice*, Second Edition. Boston, MA: Addison-Wesley, 2003.
7. Shaw M and Clements P, "The Golden Age of Software Architecture," *IEEE Software*, vol 23, no 2, March/April, 2006, pp 31–19.
8. Rowland D. and Howe TN, *Vitruvius. Ten Books on Architecture*, Cambridge: Cambridge University Press 1999.
9. Jacobson I., Griss M. and Jonsson P, *Software Reuse: Architecture, Process and Organization for Business Success*, New York: ACM Press, 1997.
10. Alexander C, *The Nature of Order An Essay on the Art of Building and the Nature of the Universe: Book III - A Vision of a Living World*, Berkeley, CA: The Center for Environmental Structure, 2005, p 4.

Chapter 11
Thriving Systems and Beauty

Christopher Alexander's framework of *living structure* exploring the form and relationships of physical architecture explains the affinity that exists between the observer and the architecture. Alexander persuasively argues that the experience of *life* demonstrated in his image comparison experiments is conveyed through a lens sensitive to 15 discernible properties that evoke an observer's sense of satisfaction in what they see. I believe that Alexander chose the term "*life*" without defining it to have each observer tap into their own visceral sense of satisfaction. Thus, Alexander's framework bridges a distance in our understanding that separates what we think of as objective design quality and what observers experience as subjective design quality, what we call beauty.

When we think of constructing or engineering systems, there is a tendency to focus on the characteristics that indicate quantitative metrics of quality – characteristics considered objective. When we think of those same systems as appealing or satisfying in terms of observer experience, we tend to focus on the characteristics of aesthetics considered subjective. Is this really a dichotomy?

11.1 "Objective" System Quality Assessment

Typically, the quality of architecture in information systems revolves around two primary concepts: efficiency and effectiveness defined as follows (all the referenced definitions provided here are taken from the New Oxford American Dictionary [1]):

efficiency [noun]- the ratio of the useful work performed by a machine or in a process to the total energy [effort] expended

effectiveness [noun]- successful in producing a desired or intended result

At first glance, these qualities appear primarily quantitative and therefore objective. And in and of themselves, they may well be. Portraying efficiency using a convenient interpretation of "work" and "effort" is genuinely objective. "How many" or "how much" or "how often" product emerges while expending "how much"

L.J. Waguespack, *Thriving Systems Theory and Metaphor-Driven Modeling*, DOI 10.1007/978-1-84996-302-2_11, © Springer-Verlag London Limited 2010

(time/money) and "how many" (work hours/workers) for "what duration" of operation often depicts efficiency. When that measure is posed against a practical question of "Is it enough?," its apparent objectivity fads away.

Likewise, considering effectiveness more deeply reveals that any supposed objectivity relies upon the tenuous phrase, "desired or intended result" defined as

intend [noun]- have (a course of action) as one's purpose or objective; plan

Effectiveness (like efficiency) is a quality of correspondence between a system and the intentions of its stakeholders. Assessing the degree of effectiveness depends on comparing "what is" to "what is intended." While the former may be expressed quantitatively, the latter presents challenges: clarity of conception, mode of representation, scope of contextual orientation, and fidelity of communication to name but a few. Indeed, the notion of effectiveness is much more complicated when we contemplate identifying and quantifying the stakeholder(s) intentions in terms we may think of as objectivity.

11.2 "Subjective" System Quality Assessment

The indefiniteness or imprecision that characterizes stakeholder intention(s) is generally not a concern if an observer is asked to assess the beauty of something – an assessment generally conceded to be subjective. A detailed or even explicit expression of intentions is not usually expected in an assessment of beauty – it is most often perceived as a reaction to an observation rather than an analysis of systems features mapped to preconceived requirements. The dictionary defines several terms relating to beauty, thus affecting an observer's experience:

beauty [noun]- a combination of qualities, such as shape, color, or form that pleases the aesthctic senses, esp. sight

please [verb]- cause to feel happy and satisfied

satisfy [verb]- meet the expectations, needs, or desires of (someone)

expectation [noun]- a belief that someone will or should achieve something

aesthetic [adjective]- concerned with beauty or the appreciation of beauty

Beauty is commonly assumed to be a subjective assessment and usually exempt from necessary, specific justification or explanation as in "Beauty is in the eye of the beholder." and "You'll know it [beauty] when you see it." This absence or difficulty in forming a quantitative justification of beauty is often the basis for categorizing artifacts or processes as products of art rather than science. This also would seem to indicate that beauty is somehow arbitrary (or in Fred Brooks' terms – accidental). And therein lies the presumption that the aspects of design quality that we label objective and those we label subjective are somehow dichotomous.

The results of Alexander's image experiments reveal that humans distinguish the degrees of *life* they observe consistently – more than 80% of the time cannot be arbitrary or accidental. This degree of consistency bespeaks a shared framework of assessment, something that causes 8 out of 10 of these observers to recognize the greater degree of *life* in one of the two images – I propose that it is appropriate to say "They recognize a greater degree of beauty."

11.3   The Experience of Quality in Observation

To understand the observer experience of quality, we need to examine the "moving parts" of the experience. Four parts of the experience are clearly present: (1) an observer's *mindset*, (2) an *expectation*, (3) a *threshold* of experience, and (4) an underlying system *implementation* (see Fig. 11.1).

The observer's *mindset* explains the "mental picture" that the observer brings to the observation.[1] This picture defines a context within which the observer will "understand" the experience and sense some degree of satisfaction. This realistically represents the personality of the observer.

The next part of the observation experience is the *expectation*. Some subset of the observer's *mindset* is specifically relevant to the observation event. It is a set of *expectations* about the observation that the observer brings to the event.[2] These *expectations* may be explicit having been formed through analysis or they may be implicit based on presumption or general predisposition. While explicit *expectations* are conscious and suitable for expression in some form of communication, this is not necessarily the case with implicit *expectations* that may be unconscious or at least in some manner unorganized and thus difficult or impossible to clearly or accurately express.

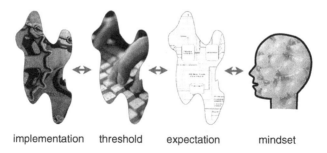

    implementation   threshold   expectation   mindset

Fig. 11.1 Four-part observation experience

---

[1] The observer's mindset is illustrated as a collection of ideas (light bulbs).

[2] Expectations are illustrated as a plan or model of requisites that "define" what the observer is "looking for" or "expects" to observe.

The third part of the observation experience is the *threshold* that constitutes the point of encounter between the observer's *expectations* and the system's features. This might be described as the ability of the system's *implementation* to "communicate" with the observer. In information systems, this might be called the user interface.[3]

Finally, there is the fourth part, the underlying *implementation* where an assembled artifact creates the opportunity of "observance." The nature and details of the *implementation* may be totally hidden from the observer if the *threshold*'s realization totally obscures it. Or the *implementation*'s composition may be totally transparent and indistinguishable from the *threshold*, or any varying degree in between.

Satisfaction and the concomitant recognition of beauty result from the observer's experience of the alignment of *expectations* with the *implementation* through the *threshold*. This encounter between the observer and the system, an observation event, realizes a degree of perceived alignment resulting in a resonance where the perception and the *expectations* seem to reinforce (or validate) one another. At some level, the resonance that the observer experiences in the encounter, the satisfaction, is interpreted as beauty:

> *beauty [noun]-* a combination of qualities, such as shape, color, or form that pleases the aesthetic senses

An observation event may be instantaneous as in a fleeting glance at a painting, a phrase of a musical melody, a line from a poem, or of long duration as in residing in a building. Satisfaction and the sense of beauty is the product of the ongoing process of encounter and interaction. Satisfaction as the product of alignment is affected by each of the four parts in the observation experience. And since each of the four elements is dynamic – satisfaction is also dynamic.

Mindset dynamics encompass all the complex ramifications of "nature and nurture."[4] There are instincts that appear to precede experience. There are changes brought on by experience and learning – the result of a life-long chain of observation events. The *mindset* is subject to all the evolutionary elements of maturation and aging.

The observation *mindset* may not be homogeneous as when the observer is a community rather than an individual (see Fig. 11.2). Understanding and expressing the *expectations* of a community is complex in itself. Although the *mindset* is the least accessible or directly controllable element of the observation experience, it is malleable (as in "developing an acquired taste for something"). *Expectations* evolve as the observer's (individual or community) *mindset* evolves.

Perhaps to a greater effect on satisfaction, the dimensionality of those *expectations* shapes the disposition toward satisfaction. This dimensionality may be likened to

---

[3]The threshold is illustrated as a keyboard or keystrokes as one might need to learn to exercise the communication between observer and system implementation.

[4]Nature versus nurture refers to the long standing debates concerning the degree to which life is shaped more or less predominantly by innate qualities ("nature") versus experiences ("nurture") in determining or causing individual differences in physical and behavioral traits.

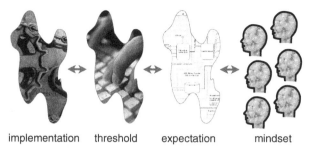

implementation   threshold   expectation   mindset

Fig. 11.2 Observer as community

"degrees of freedom" where some aspects of an observation experience are held to tight criteria while others are effectively ignored. Narrow, simple *expectations* based on a few explicit needs or desires will plausibly align with a relatively few elements in the *threshold* making satisfaction rather straightforward and probable. As the number of dimensions grows in the *expectation*, so grows the difficulty of reaching a satisfactory alignment with the *threshold*. If the *expectations* span over long-term observation events and include the observer's ability to change or control the evolution of the *implementation* and/or the *threshold*, the number of potential element alignments grows quickly and a sense of satisfaction becomes ever more complex. As with any cognitive activity, complexity raises the desire for simplification and the use of approximation and/or abstraction to render the alignment intellectually tractable.[5]

The *threshold* impacts satisfaction through its capacity to be recognized as addressing elements of the *expectation* and to give access to the *implementation* elements that fulfill that *expectation*. Many observers (e.g. end-users) are only concerned with the *threshold* to the extent that it fulfills their operational requirements and thus are solely concerned with this aspect of system functionality. They are not interested in long-term maintenance, system evolution, or cost of ownership beyond their own individual transaction costs. Their needs represent only a narrow slice of the *expectation* dimensionality addressed earlier. On occasion, the *threshold*'s representation may tap into the observers' latent *expectations* and in so doing alter the *mindset* by emphasizing or suggesting new aspects of *expectation*. In this situation, *expectation* is at least partially based on the opportunity offered by the *threshold* rather than the observers' preexisting "need."[6] In any case, the *threshold* as the focal point of the observation encounter cannot be overestimated in its importance in enabling satisfaction.

The *implementation* part of the observation experience tends to focus on *expectation* dimensions set by investors, owners, builders, and custodians of the

---

[5]Hence, the reference to "imprecision" earlier to stakeholder intentions where the effort required to maintain a precise expression of the expectations is deemed too "expensive" and detail is reduced by some means.

[6]This is the basic tenet of marketing: "Create a need by posing an opportunity."

system more so than the users who may feel free of these concerns. Although usually hidden by the *threshold*, the *implementation* is sensitive to the *expectations* of the observers responsible for the cost of availability, reliability, and serviceability. *Implementation* draws more attention to cost and efficiency as these may reflect a greater opportunity for flexibility and options than the *expectations* of clients or users. It is interesting to note that in those observation events usually thought of as artistic in nature, a focus on *implementation* recedes far into the background of concerns. While in events normally thought to be construction or engineering in nature, the focus on *implementation* receives much more attention to an apparent relative diminution of a concern for beauty.

In the end, the only real difference between quality purportedly assessed objectively versus subjectively is in the granularity with which we inspect the four parts in an observation event. Perhaps, we deem assessments of quality to be subjective simply because we do not subject them to rigorous dissection and the assignment of constituent significance, metrics. Subjective quality assessments appear more arbitrary because they are more complex than the analytical effort we choose to invest.

11.4 Is It Beauty or Is It Thriving?

In this discussion of observable quality, again it becomes clear that design is only a part of quality systems. The key is the synergy that must exist between the understanding of "what the system should do" and "what and how the system does do." The beauty in systems results as the implemented system's capabilities resonate with the stakeholder community's shared understanding of their *expectations*. This can only occur when a "high-quality" formulation and expression of stakeholder *expectations* spanning the dimensions of construction, effectiveness, efficiency, and evolution is complimented by an implemented design that fulfills those *expectations*.

Alexander's *center* properties translated to *choice* properties expose the fundamental elements of order that shape form and relationships to produce structures and processes that achieve beauty. The 15 *choice* properties explicitly apply to the *implementation*, the *threshold*, and the *expectation* of the observation experience. The *choice* properties expose the synergy of form and relationships that both shape individual building blocks and explain how those blocks when brought together fuse into a *wholeness* that successively enfolds their individuality in a recursion of composition and abstraction.

Lakoff's description of human cognition and knowledge explains that the cascade of abstraction that the *choice* enfolding process entails not only coincides with but mirrors the structure of human understanding, communication, and learning. The matrix of abstractions mirrors that of the conceptual metaphors that capture and catalog concepts, both objective and subjective. As a result, Lakoff explains *mindset* and the phenomenon of resonance felt as beauty. Both matrices represent an inexhaustible resource of variation and combination of alternative *choices* with which to refine or strengthen the whole.

Brooks' theory provides a device for escaping the infinity of *choice* decisions by characterizing choices as *essence* or *accident*. This is the opportunity to balance effectiveness with feasibility. Conceptual metaphors and the abstractions that represent them achieve a partitioning of reality that makes an approximation of reality feasible. The levels of approximation and feasibility achieved depend on the cost versus the benefit intentions of the stakeholders.

The nexus of *choice* properties, conceptual metaphors, and a criterion for designating *choices* as either *essence* or *accident* forms the framework for characterizing the beauty in systems. This framework informs the process of conceiving and communicating observer *expectation*. It informs the process of forming and aligning a *threshold* to those *expectations*. And it guides the development of an *implementation* to realize the functionality conveyed through the *threshold*. It does this by drawing on the innate organization of knowledge and understanding of the observer, the *mindset*. This framework designates a *thriving system*: a collection of *choices* exhibiting strong, balanced *choice* properties, clearly expressing *essence* and *accident*, while representing a recognized conceptual metaphor of the stakeholders' *expectation*.[7] The stakeholder community experiences a resonance of the system's properties with their anticipation of *strength* and *functionality* [2]. A *thriving system* is a thing of beauty!

References

1. McKean E (editor), *The New Oxford American Dictionary*, Second Edition, 2051 p, Oxford University Press, New York, May 2005.
2. Rowland D and Howe TN, *Vitruvius. Ten Books on Architecture*. Cambridge University Press, Cambridge, 1999.

---

[7]See Section 10.7.

Chapter 12
Promoting *Life* Using the Object-Oriented Paradigm

The concepts of system ecology and *life*-preserving transformations presented thus far can be integrated into any building process where *choices* are made. To illustrate, this chapter describes how these concepts can be realized in and are facilitated by the object-oriented paradigm and engineering processes associated with it. It is not the object-oriented paradigm's uniqueness in offering these modeling concepts that sets it apart – for the paradigm has borrowed almost all its concepts from other approaches. But rather, it is the coincidence of concepts in a single paradigm that offers such a pleasingly ingenious and expressive tool for expressing *life*.

As a first step in this illustration, the defining characteristics of the object-oriented paradigm must be shifted from the popular experience of developers immersed in the *accidents of implementation* accompanying most of the programming languages and development tools commonly used to implement object-oriented artifacts. The discussion begins with an ontology describing the paradigm's concepts and its vocabulary [1]. That is followed up by a review of each of the *life-preserving choice* properties and the opportunity that the object-oriented paradigm provides for incorporating them.

12.1   An Ontology of the Object-Oriented Paradigm

This ontology is consistent with the practice in computer science and information science categorizing a domain of concepts (i.e. individuals, attributes, relationships, and classes). This ontology of the object-oriented paradigm attempts to eschew the vestiges of implementation languages and development methodologies to expose the core nature and value of object-oriented concepts (Fig. 12.1).

The object-oriented ontology is arranged as follows:

1. Individuals
2. Attributes

    (a) Data Attributes
    (b) Behavioral Attributes

3. Classes

L.J. Waguespack, *Thriving Systems Theory and Metaphor-Driven Modeling*,
DOI 10.1007/978-1-84996-302-2_12, © Springer-Verlag London Limited 2010

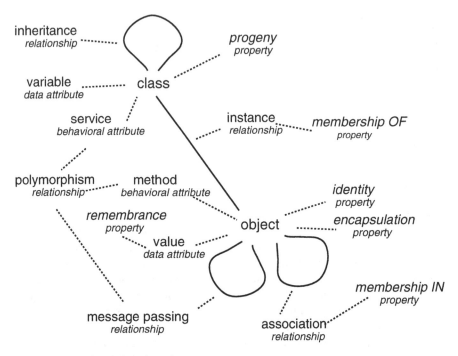

Fig. 12.1 The object-oriented ontology

4. Relationships

   (a) Structural Relationships
      • Inheritance
   (b) Behavioral Relationships

      • Association
      • Message Passing
      • Polymorphism

Individuals – The most concrete concept in the object-oriented paradigm is the object. It derives from the living physical experience of humans seeing and touching things. In that experience, objects are separable – distinguishable from other objects by nature of their physical presence and location regardless of any other discernible characteristics they may possess. This characteristic of "individual-ness" leads to the property of identity. Identity enables the unambiguous designation or selection of every object, physical or abstract, within a domain of discourse. Objects have an "inside," an "outside," and a "surface" that separates the inside from the outside. An object contains anything that exists on the "inside" of the object. Since the surface of most physical objects is opaque, usually the contents are invisible and untouchable by anyone on the outside. This property called encapsulation protects the object's contents from external meddling and encourages observers of the object to be indifferent to the details of its internals.

Attributes – Attributes are those characteristics that are inherent to an object. In the object paradigm, attributes define either data or behavioral characteristics – each of which has a static and dynamic form. Attributes in static form combine to define what is called the structure of an object. From inception to extinction, the structure of an object is immutable.

Data Attributes – Data attributes serve to store information (data) within an object and implement the property of remembrance. Data attributes are completely contained within an object protected by encapsulation. Remembrance is manifest statically as "what can be remembered," a data attribute variable. It is manifest dynamically as a definition of "what is remembered," a particular data attribute value.

Behavioral Attributes – Behavioral attributes serve to define the animate nature of an object. In its static form, each behavioral attribute defines "what an object can do," usually called a service. In its corresponding dynamic form, this behavioral attribute defines "how a service is accomplished," usually called a method (or operation). Methods define "activity" performed in an object model. A method may simply be access to remembrance inside an object or it may be complex sometimes employing the involvement of other services of the same or other objects to accomplish its responsibility. Methods reside within the object subject to encapsulation while services are visible at the surface of the object available for collaboration.

Classes – The class concept combines both a definition of structure and the generation of object(s) based on that structure. Every object is an instance of a specific class and shares the same static structure defined by that class with every other object of that class. The responsibility of generating instances that share the same structure is the property of progeny. The class concept thereby fuses the existence of the objects to that of their class; objects cannot exist independent of their defining class. Objects are said to be members OF their class. Along with the static behavioral structure of service defined in the class, the dynamic behavioral attribute, method, may also be defined. Defined in the class, this dynamic behavioral attribute, "how a service is accomplished," is identical for each and every object generated of that class.

Relationships – Relationships in the object paradigm exist on two dimensions: structural and behavioral.

Structural Relationships – The structural relationship is based primarily on the properties of identity, remembrance, and progeny.

Inheritance – Inheritance is a relationship between classes. The structure defined in one class is used as the foundation of structure in another. By foundation, it is meant that all the structure of the first is replicated in the second and additional structure in terms of data attributes or services may be added or methods for replicated services may be altered (overridden). The replicated structure defines how the two classes are alike. The additions or alterations define how they are different. The class defining all the structure shared between them is called the parent class (superclass, generalization) while the other is called the child class (subclass, specialization). It is said that the child class proceeds from or is derived from the parent class. Successive application of inheritance defining related classes results in a class hierarchy.

Behavioral Relationships – The behavioral relationships are based primarily on the property of membership IN and the capacity of objects to "act."

Association – An association is a relationship between objects. Objects are intrinsically separable by way of the identity property. At the same time, humans are compelled to categorize their experience of things in the physical world. Humans superimpose groupings that collect objects into sets (a foundation of mathematics based on human experience [2]). Objects become members in a group only by designation. This property is called membership IN. Membership is independent of identity or attribute. This property also permits humans to identify an object that is not in a set (i.e. discrimination). (Membership IN a group is discretionary and is distinct from membership OF a class, which is intrinsic by way of progeny.) Variations on membership derive from the intent of the relationship and generally fall into the categories of association and composition. Any designated collection of objects defines a relationship between those objects called association. By the simple fact that they are members in the same relationship that membership defines how they relate. When the existence of the objects themselves is coupled with their member-ship, that is to say, if one (or the other or both) would not exist if it were not related to the other, then the relationship is called a composition.

Message Passing – Message passing is a relationship between objects. Message pass-ing relies on the identity property and services. A message is a communication between a sender object and receiver object where the sender requests that the receiver render one of its services. The sender and receiver may be one in the same object. The message designates the receiver's identity, the receiver's service to be performed along with any parameters that the service's protocol may require. Since the message is a request, there are no implicit timing constraints determining when the service is accomplished. Unless explicitly designated, a message results in an asynchronous activity on the part of the receiver without acknowledgment or returned information.

Polymorphism – Polymorphism results from the interplay of message passing, behavioral attributes, and classes. A sender directs a message to a receiver designating a service of that receiver. The same service name may exist in multiple classes of the same or distinct class hierarchies. A message does not designate a method. The regime that determines which method satisfies a service request is called binding. If the method (corresponding to the service) is defined in the class of the receiver object, that method is invoked. If the service of the receiver's class is inherited (and not overridden), the corresponding method defined in the nearest progenitor (parent class) of the receiving object's class is invoked.

12.2   Modeling Living Structure in the Object-Oriented Paradigm

Chapter 3 recounted Christopher Alexander's theories of *wholeness* and *centers* explaining that the degree of *wholeness* derives from the strength or intensity that each *center* contributes to the whole. The strength or intensity of a *center* results from the intensity of the various 15 properties that he attributes to the *centers*. Recall that *centers* were recast as *choices* to map Alexander's theories of physical architecture

Table 12.1 Properties of *Centers* mapped to *Choice* properties

	Alexander's property	1	2	3	4	5	6	7	8	9	10	11	12	13	14	15	Choice property
1	Levels of Scale		*	*			*			*							Stepwise Refinement
2	Strong Centers			*			*		*	*			*		*		Cohesion
3	Boundaries		*		*			*	*	*	*						Encapsulation
4	Alternating Repetition		*			*	*		*	*					*		Extensibility
5	Positive Space	*	*	*			*	*		*		*		*			Modularization
6	Good Shape	*	*			*	*		*		*		*		*		Correctness
7	Local Symmetries	*				*			*				*				Transparency
8	Deep Interlock and Ambiguity				*	*			*		*	*				*	Composition of Function
9	Contrast			*		*		*		*			*		*		Identity
10	Gradients	*	*				*		*		*	*			*		Scale
11	Roughness		*		*	*				*				*	*		User Friendliness
12	Echoes	*				*	*			*	*				*		Patterns
13	The Void	*		*		*	*	*						*			Programmability
14	Simplicity and Inner Calm					*	*					*	*		*		Reliability
15	Not Separateness			*		*		*		*	*		*	*			Elegance

onto the domain of information systems, their models, and architecture. Table 12.1 reproduces Table 3.1 for the reader's convenience. Table 12.1 summarizes the 15 properties and their interrelationships along with corresponding *choice* properties [3].

The following addresses each of the *choice* properties in turn and examines how each property relates to and is in fact facilitated by the object-oriented paradigm. As these items derive from Alexander's property list, which was parsed from an experience of physical architecture, it is not surprising that the items in this list are often deeply interwoven in the promotion of *life* in the more abstract world of information systems.

12.2.1 Stepwise Refinement

Stepwise Refinement reliant upon Cohesion, Encapsulation, Correctness, and Identity (derived from Levels of Scale reliant upon Strong Centers, Boundaries, Good Shape, and Contrast) incorporated in the choice by the modeling action "to elaborate:"

As the name implies, *stepwise refinement* is an approach to model elaboration that presumes that a problem should be addressed in stages. The stages may represent degrees of detail or an expanding scope of problem coverage. In either case, the goal of *stepwise refinement* is to demonstrate a cogent and complete representation of the modeling solution at whatever level of detail or scope that has been set for this stage. To achieve this, the representation (the paradigm) must support abstraction that allows generalization of the scope of interest and then the elaboration of that scope from one stage to the next.

In the object paradigm, the class concept provides this capability. Through generalization/specialization, a class can represent the more abstract, general character of a model feature while expressing all the information and behavior that would be evident at that level of abstraction: (1) what responsibilities will be fulfilled by objects of this class, (2) what information will they be responsible for managing, and (3) what services can the rest of the objects in the model expect this class's objects to provide. As the modeling stages progress, greater specialization may be achieved either by creating child classes that redefine the abstract behaviors targeted to more specific application by adding data and/or behavior attributes germane only at a lower level of abstraction, or by defining collaborations to support this class's responsibilities. *Stepwise Refinement* can mimic the concept of "need-to-know." Only that detail at that level of abstraction required to "understand" the system needs to be revealed or perhaps that detail is not even chosen until the need arises. When the need does arise, the detail may be added within the genealogy of the class preserving the *cohesion* of functional responsibility defined in the class at the highest abstraction level.

As an example, consider a class that defines items stored in an inventory. At the most general level, the most important functional detail is the entry and removal of items. As refinement continues, simple entry and removal may be augmented by including item re-order and supplier interaction both concealed from the inventory item's client in its expanded behavior of entry and removal. The supplier interaction details are *encapsulated* within the inventory item's responsibilities retaining the *cohesion* of the class's responsibilities (its *identity*). And the description of the inventory item exhibits *correctness* at either level of detail with or without the supplier interaction defined.

12.2.2   Cohesion

Cohesion reliant upon Extensibility, Transparency, Identity, Scale, Programmability, and Elegance (derived from Strong Centers reliant upon Alternating Repetition, Local Symmetries, Contrast, Gradients, The Void, and Not Separateness) incorporated in the choice by the modeling action "to factor:"

Cohesion derived from *strong centers* reflects the consistency of responsibility distribution in a field of system components. Since every object "expects" the objects around it to fulfill their responsibilities to contribute to the whole, each object is in itself free to be single-minded in its focus on its own purpose. This is the result of well-chosen classes. This independent sufficiency accentuates the divisibility of function both in terms of each object's individual purpose, its *identity*, and in terms of the clarity with which its purpose is exposed to the rest of the community of objects in the system. The single-mindedness that results also increases the feasibility of object interaction rearrangement enabling an overall change in system function while almost every class's individual purpose remains fixed. The independent sufficiency of each object's inner workings couples with the systemwide interdependency of object cooperation to promote a texture exhibiting a sense of system connectedness, *elegance*.

12.2.3 Encapsulation

Encapsulation reliant upon Cohesion, Extensibility, Transparency, Composition of Function, Identity, and Scale (derived from Boundaries reliant upon Strong Centers, Alternating Repetition, Local Symmetries, Deep Interlock and Ambiguity, Contrast, and Gradients) incorporated in the choice by the modeling action "to encapsulate:"

By the nature of the object-oriented ontology, objects *encapsulate* both their data and behavioral attributes. *Encapsulation* clearly delineates who is allowed to manipulate system information and who is not. Object data and behavior are only accessible (invokable) via the published services defined for each object by its class. When sustained as a discipline, this boundary universally designates the object as the finest granule of *modularization*. This principle eliminates the possibility of "side effects" where system state changes in any manner other than the "contractual" prescription defined in the object's service interface. The isolation of the inside of the object from the outside allows both to evolve without servitude to the implementation of either (as in the pursuit of efficiency) as an object is obligated only through the published responsibilities in its class's services.

(Regrettably, *encapsulation* as an object-oriented property is often diluted in implementation as something with far less integrity than it is defined here. Excused by arguments for efficiency or convenience access to object attributes by means other than the contractual interface of services defined in the object's class creates "back doors" that confound testing and render *composition of function* hazardous.)

12.2.4 Extensibility

Extensibility reliant upon Cohesion, Modularization, Correctness, Composition of Function, Identity, and Elegance (derived from Alternating Repetition reliant upon Strong Centers, Positive Space, Good Shape, Deep Interlock and Ambiguity, Contrast, and Not Separateness) incorporated in the choice by the modeling action "to render extendable:"

Of all the characteristics that may exist in a modeling paradigm, *extensibility* may be the most important in pursuing systems with *life*. This is the vehicle for seamless *unfolding* in system evolution. In the object-oriented paradigm, class plays the pivotal role by empowering instance and inheritance relationships.

Multiplicity is achieved through instance propagation, *progeny*. Each instance is completely interoperable in any combination with its sibling objects as well as acting as an instance of any ancestor class. Interchangeability both enables and reinforces *modularization.*

Evolution or *unfolding* is accomplished as class definitions are refined and specialized in their child classes – the relationship called *inheritance.* When a child class extends the scope of the data and behavioral attributes of its parent, it honors the pattern set out in the parent without contradiction. *Polymorphism* compensates (through dynamic binding) for any overridden methods. This extension proceeds without any impairment of *correctness* because the interfaces defined in the parent class must be supported in each child class. The parent to child *unfolding* specializing structure and behavior results in an unbroken thread that binds the lineage to its ancestry and projects an *identity* through the generations of class.

12.2.5 Modularization

> Modularization reliant upon Stepwise Refinement, Cohesion, Encapsulation, Correctness, Transparency, Identity, User Friendliness, and Programmability (derived from Positive Space reliant upon Levels of Scale, Strong Centers, Boundaries, Good Shape, Local Symmetries, Contrast, Roughness, and The Void) incorporated in the choice by the modeling action "to modularize:"

Along with *cohesion*, this principle of *modularization* enables "divide and conquer" problem-solving augmented by the flexibility of configuring and reconfiguring objects as cooperating agents. *Modularization* also supports *scale* permitting the composition of subsystems of varying scope that holds details in abeyance until they require focus. Enlightened module design exposes the solution structure envisioned by the modeler and publishes intentions for further extension by separation of concerns and isolation of *accidents of implementation.* The object-oriented paradigm provides ample facility for defining modules of any size and scope while aggregating and/or nesting their interfaces through deliberate information hiding. The granularity enabled through *modularization* may be applied to facilitate the modeler's formulation of structure as well as the perspective to aid stakeholder recognition and understanding.

12.2.6 Correctness

> Correctness reliant upon Stepwise Refinement, Cohesion, Modularization, Correctness, Composition of Function, Scale, Patterns, and Reliability (derived from Good Shape reliant upon Levels of Scale, Strong Centers, Positive Space, Good Shape, Deep Interlock and Ambiguity, Gradients, Echoes, and Simplicity and Inner Calm) incorporated in the choice by the modeling action "to align:"

Information system *correctness* depends heavily upon two outcomes: (1) the clarity and fidelity of the represented understanding of system characteristics, *validation* and (2) the completeness and effectiveness of model feature testing both individually and in composition, *verification*.

Validation depends on the fidelity of the *unfolding* process; through the stages of *stepwise refinement* the *essential* aspects of system characteristics are brought forward maintaining their integrity. *Modularization* aids in cataloging and focusing on individual *essential* characteristics. *Choices* in the earliest stages of *unfolding* will be the signature for each of their *unfoldings* that follow and thus *correctness* is recursive. *Correctness* is the only *choice* property that supports itself! *Correctness* must be a priority at each stage as experience shows that *correctness* shortcomings grow more and more expensive to rehabilitate as evolution progresses – notice "rehabilitate," to restore to normal *life*.

Verification depends on the effective testability of each *choice* to certify it as "consistent with stakeholder understanding." *Modularization* aides in the verification of individual *choices* or modules and then relying on the *correctness* inside modules verification can turn to the certification of behaviors resulting from *composition of function*. Experience often leads to dependable *patterns* of classes or modules that can be adapted and applied to recurring modeling tasks. Verification in these situations can focus on known areas of fragility/risk and thus limit the effort required to reach a desired level of *reliability*. The class hierarchy by itself may be the best example of applying *patterns* to models.

12.2.7 Transparency

Transparency reliant upon Stepwise Refinement, Modularization, Identity, and Programmability (derived from Local Symmetries reliant upon Levels of Scale, Positive Space, Contrast, and The Void) incorporated in the choice by the modeling action "to expose:"

The key here is evident structure, revealing how things fit and work together. In the object-oriented paradigm, "fit together" and "work together" are defined by the structural and behavioral relationships. Individual objects may represent clearly delineated and encapsulated *choices*, but their cooperation is defined by relationships.

Inheritance explains the structural relationship of classes through the propagation of the structure of data and behavioral attributes. Inheritance not only propagates attributes but also enables a class hierarchy's capacity for exhibiting similarity and difference between parent and child classes. That which is similar (in fact identical) inherited by the child class is assumed and becomes in effect familiar – requiring no reiteration. This "folding" of that which is not changed avoids clutter in the child class description, but may be readily reviewed in the parent.

The behavioral relationships of association, message passing, and polymorphism explain the predictable *patterns* of communication and action. Association uses the property of *identity* to designate membership, ownership, and accessibility among objects. Message passing provides the mechanism for cooperating action between objects providing a disciplined conduit through the boundary of objects by using services to convey intention, information, and reaction. Polymorphism allows the abstraction of intention by using the same service reference to evoke distinct responses when applied to objects of different classes. The identical service names in classes with different methods directly realize the metaphorical abstraction of object behavior where at one level of abstraction the behaviors are the same and at a more detailed level of abstraction their behaviors are distinct.

These connections form a pattern describing what is possible in the relationship. Together, they expose a prescription of potential occurrences and interconnectedness that bound what can happen (the possible) and leave what may happen to the instant (the occurrence).

12.2.8 Composition of Function

Composition of Function reliant upon Extensibility, Modularization, Identity, User Friendliness, Patterns, and Programmability (derived from Deep Interlock and Ambiguity reliant upon Alternating Repetition, Positive Space, Contrast, Roughness, Echoes, and The Void) incorporated in the choice by the modeling action "to assemble:"

As a fundamental tool for managing complexity, humans regularly attempt to decompose problems, issues, or tasks into parts that either in themselves are sufficiently simple to permit direct solution or can through recursion be subdivided again until they become sufficiently simple. This is a defining aspect of *modularization*. When the conception of the parts also anticipates reuse, then the part takes on a larger significance. The combination of specifying a *choice* consistent with the *essence* of system characteristics and then designing the *choice* as an interchangeable component in multiple superordinate *choices* is a step toward *elegance*. Reusable *choices* represent an understanding of the *essence* of the system at a deeper level than an individual application. They represent awareness of the intention, perhaps even the philosophy of the system domain. (Achieving this "awareness" is a primary goal of the object-oriented software engineering activity called domain analysis.) In a sense, this principle is the dual of "divide-and-conquer," it is "constitute-and-compose."

Composition of function as a principle is realized in model features that facilitate the extension or retargeting of the model in the future. The retargeting capability may be provided directly to the users of the system in the form of a *programmable* interface. A *choice* achieving the principle of *composition of function* is marked not only by the function it initially provides the user, but also by the functionality it anticipates and supports even (perhaps) *before* the stakeholders decide to engage the capability.

Many examples of *composition of function* exist in software – the whole range of tools and features that support reuse: programming macros, application frameworks, module libraries, component frameworks, and web services are a few. All these examples may be readily achieved using inheritance, class hierarchies, and polymorphism in the object-oriented paradigm.

12.2.9 Identity

Identity reliant upon Encapsulation, Modularization, Composition of Function, Scale, Programmability, and Elegance (derived from Contrast reliant upon Boundaries, Positive Space, Deep Interlock and Ambiguity, Gradients, The Void, and Not Separateness) incorporated in the choice by the modeling action "to identify:"

Identity is at the root of recognition. In the physical world, *identity* is literal based on direct sensorimotor experience: by sight or touch and in some cases by sound or smell – a human experience of the "real" world. In the object-oriented paradigm, *identity* is an object property. Existence is sufficient for object identification.

In other paradigms, identification is achieved through possessed characteristics (attributes) that contribute to distinct recognition by a process of intersecting categorizations or the introduction of an artificial characteristic whose sole purpose is to support discrimination. Aside from the fact that these approaches to identification require some overhead (either mental or computational), they are simply not natural to humans. Humans perceive objects as possessing characteristics rather than characteristics defining objects. The former begins with certain uniqueness and progresses toward explanation while the latter begins with uncertainty and attempts to deduce uniqueness.

Characteristics are not unimportant. Classification is essential in most human problem-solving activities. And recognition is virtually always accelerated by the discrimination that categorizing characteristics (attributes) provide. And most importantly, in the absence of physical experience, categorization through characteristics is the only choice. Class structure and the instance relationship are vital to *identity* – an object belongs to "this" class and not to "another." Described both by what an object "knows" (data attributes) and what it "knows how to do" (behavioral attributes), classes form a categorization cornerstone of the object-oriented ontology. But to model both the static and dynamic dimensions of reality (association and message passing), each object must be uniquely distinguishable.

Clarity of *identity* is not served well by multiple-inheritance, however. The assimilation of characteristics from two (or more) parent classes complicates the human activity of recognition. The natural classification process is at least slowed if not confounded by objects of multiple-inheritance, objects that are "neither fish nor fowl!" In this writing, it is not justified to say that multiple-inheritance is a provable violation of the preservation of *life*; however, it is clear that multiple-inheritance is not the property of *deep interlock and ambiguity* that Alexander ascribes to architecture with *life*. It is this author's strong opinion that when characteristics from more than one class need to be collocated for an *essential* reason, then in every case association is superior to multiple-inheritance with no loss in expression and a marked increase in clarity.

12.2.10 Scale

Scale reliant upon Stepwise Refinement, Cohesion, Transparency, Identity, User Friendliness, Patterns, and Elegance (derived from Gradients reliant upon Levels of Scale, Strong Centers, Local Symmetries, Contrast, Roughness, Echoes, and Not Separateness) incorporated in the choice by the modeling action "to focus:"

The affect of *scale* is reflected in a couple of common idioms: "You can't see the forest for the trees!" and "Let's get a view from 10,000 feet." They reflect the importance of context in recognition and decision-making. Alexander's focus on the whole composed of a *field* of strong *centers* is reflected in the *choice* property of *scale*. *Scale* captures the modeling imperative that all *choices* must be kept in perspective because it is not sufficient to consider a *choice* only in the microcosm of itself, as it must also participate in the connectedness of the whole.

The relationships provided in the object-oriented paradigm (association, inheritance, instance, message passing, and even polymorphism) provide ample means for designing collections of cooperating *choices* that are nested, intersect, or partition the full *field* of functionality *essential* to the model. These may be called variously subsystems, modules, or submodules. In those cases where the actual structure of a collection must be rendered obscure, classes and objects can be devised to serve as facades or agents to "keep up appearances." Coupled with *stepwise refinement* as it is, *scale* is used to focus modeler and stakeholder attention to achieve the contextual understanding needed to address constituent concerns within the whole.

12.2.11   User Friendliness

> User Friendliness reliant upon Cohesion, Modularization, Correctness, Scale, Reliability, and Elegance (derived from Roughness reliant upon Strong Centers, Positive Space, Good Shape, Gradients, Simplicity and Inner Calm, and Not Separateness) incorporated in the choice by the modeling action "to accommodate:"

To understand the impact of *user friendliness*, it may be easiest to consider its absence. A modeling *choice* that is unfriendly to users is confusing, hard to comprehend, unwieldy, and perhaps worst of all of indeterminate *correctness*. That which defies understanding fails to exhibit *life*. Stakeholder-satisfying processes produce stakeholder-satisfying models. Satisfaction is cumulative. The sensitivity to the stakeholders' conceptions of the *essence* of the system to be modeled is key to Alexander's *life-preserving process* of *unfolding*.

The object-oriented paradigm excels in its facility to represent systems characteristics in a way that preserves the stakeholders' ability to recognize "their" system. Authoring abstract models in objects that correspond almost one-to-one with the real-world concepts and entities makes the object-oriented paradigm intrinsically easier to understand and interact with. The casting of "objects" in the models that have direct counterparts in the stakeholders' experience exhibits a fundamentally friendly quality. It respects the stakeholders' perceptions and it welcomes them into the processes of verification and validation that are intrinsic to *correctness*. The unified structure of "what an object knows" and "what an object knows how to do" correlates so naturally with observers of business models or process models that the natural clarity in that communication improves understanding and diminishes the proclivity for mistaken understanding, communication, or implementation.

And in a serendipitous quirk of language (or a profound emergence of the deep meaning of metaphors), Alexander's term from which the principle here, *user friendliness*, is derived is *roughness*. Something has to have a certain degree of *roughness* if one is to be able to effectively grasp it!

12.2.12 Patterns

> Patterns reliant upon Stepwise Refinement, Correctness, Transparency, Scale, User Friendliness, and Elegance (derived from Echoes reliant upon Levels of Scale, Good Shape, Local Symmetries, Gradients, Roughness, and Not Separateness) incorporated in the choice by the modeling action "to pattern:"

All actors in the object-oriented paradigm propagate from classes, predefined templates, or "cookie cutters." This protocol organizes what otherwise would be a bewildering multiplicity of individual computational entities to consider. It becomes less complicated in the understanding that the potential of any number of objects boils down to understanding the class of which they are instances. Each instance mimics perfectly the form and function of every other of its siblings, members of that class. Class hierarchies, generations of parent-child class definitions, defining "nearly the same" and "different in specific ways" relationships significantly lessen the apparent complexity that considering only individual entities entails. Class hierarchies define the path of *unfolding* for all to see – a depiction of the analysis, solution, and design philosophies at work.

Patterns channel change. They foreshadow where and how change will need to be accounted for. *Patterns* of the form popularized by Coplein et al. [4] document commonly encountered design questions offering carefully considered advice and cautions. Their patterns are paradigm and modeling language independent. However, it is not surprising that many examples using *patterns* are presented in object-oriented dialects. The reason is simple. The integration of instance, inheritance, message passing, and polymorphism relationships is an ideal toolset for expressing *patterns* with a balance of prescription and adaptability – a balance not as conveniently achieved in dialects based on pre-object-oriented paradigms.

12.2.13 Programmability

> Programmability reliant upon Stepwise Refinement, Encapsulation, Modularization, Transparency, Identity, and Reliability (derived from The Void reliant upon Levels of Scale, Boundaries, Positive Space, Local Symmetries, Contrast, and Simplicity and Inner Calm) incorporated in the choice by the modeling action "to generalize:"

Closely allied with *extensibility* above, *programmability* addresses the need for models to welcome the future. What largely separates information systems from other human-made mechanisms is the degree of adaptability that they offer to deal gracefully with change. Unlike most appliances that support a very narrow range of use (albeit with great *reliability*), contemporary information systems are expected to provide not only amplification of effort as in computation or transaction processing, but also amplification of opportunity in terms of different approaches to business, organizational, or *life* questions. Contemporary information systems are expected to demonstrate that they can reliably accommodate change. As with *extensibility*, successful accommodation of change relies on an understanding of the fundamental options governing the structure and behavior within a particular domain. The object-oriented ontology offers powerful tools (structural and behavioral relationships, e.g. inheritance and polymorphism) to service the elements of change without fracturing a skeletal foundation of base classes characterizing the domain.

What sets *programmability* apart from *extensibility* is a facility that permits altering the systems behavior without having to reconstruct *choices*. That is to say that the system's behavior can be sensitive to the context determined by a "user" in "real time." "Real time" is relative to the "user's" role (e.g. developer or end-user, etc.). This versatility is not accidental but planned.

Individual classes may define function or policy for a developer reflecting the business model, business process, information process, or even computing process levels. Objects of these classes, *encapsulated* compartments of functional and technical knowledge, provide developers the opportunity to conceive of a system as a collection of "toy parts." These "toy parts" are capable of combination and recombination in configurations yielding new and different applications often without adding components, but simply by rearranging the existing ones. For the end–users, *choices* may provide an interface language that permits selections of system actions to meet an immediate "real-time" need – an interface as simple as a light switch or as complex as a natural language.

12.2.14   *Reliability*

> Reliability reliant upon Correctness, Transparency, Patterns, Programmability, and Elegance (derived from Simplicity and Inner Calm reliant upon Good Shape, Local Symmetries, Echoes, The Void, and Not Separateness) incorporated in the choice by the modeling action "to normalize:"

Objects facilitate modularized testing and quality assurance. A certified class produces certified objects (which is not to say that certification is easy or inexpensive). As long as classes are protected from dynamic modification in deployment, there is no need to be concerned with the inner workings of their objects. As long as objects are truly *encapsulated*, they conform to the intention of their class. In development, testing proceeds incrementally as new classes are added or rearranged in their collaboration. Once deployed, testing is relegated to their interactions rather than their definition. Testing is compartmentalized and does not explode exponentially when additional classes or functionality within a class is added.

Reliability cannot ignore intention. Regardless of the paradigm, the fidelity with which the *essence* is propagated through the *unfolding* models remains primarily the intellectual responsibility of the stakeholder community rather than a modeling task. The modeling task, however, should not confound it. And in fact, the reliable reflection of stakeholder intentions should aid in the certification of those intentions as they are realized in the model proposing to express them. In that sense, the model is normalized with the stakeholders' intentions.

12.2.15 Elegance

Elegance reliant upon Encapsulation, Modularization, Composition of Function, Scale, User Friendliness, Programmability, and Reliability (derived from Not Separateness reliant upon Boundaries, Positive Space, Deep Interlock and Ambiguity, Gradients, Roughness, The Void, and Simplicity and Inner Calm) incorporated in the choice by the modeling action "to coordinate:"

"Pleasing grace and style in appearance or manner," that is how the dictionary expresses the meaning of "elegance" [5]. Models composed of *choices* that are consistent, clear, concise, coherent, cogent, and transparently correct exude *elegance* and nurture cooperation, constructive criticism, and stakeholder community confidence. These are models that confess to their own shortcomings because their clarity obscures nothing, even omissions. These are models that satisfy stakeholders. They appear "intuitively obvious." The clarity of their composite structure is so self-evident that they seem "simple." The use of the object-oriented paradigm to construct a collection of "building blocks" in the form of a class library to encapsulate architectural design decisions facilitates this impression of what is "intuitively obvious." Using well-conceived library elements becomes so second nature, so natural, that the builder perceives the blocks as the natural primitives of construction rather than constructed artifacts.

Elegance largely proceeds from the efficient and effective representation of *essential* system characteristics along with those features emerging out of design decisions, *accidents of implementation,* that are laid out with equal clarity for separate consideration. This is the *field effect* of the beneficial, integrated, mutual support of strong *choices* as Alexander describes it [3, p. 119].

12.3 Programming Languages Versus Ontology

The object-oriented ontology readily supports the 15 properties of *choices* derived from Christopher Alexander's theory of *wholeness* and *life*. All the elements of system development distinguished by Fred Brooks' as *essence* and *accidents of implementation* can be realized efficiently and explicitly in the object-oriented paradigm. The isolation of volatile requirements, technologies, interfaces, etc. can be managed to eliminate as much as possible unintended maintenance due to intermingling of requirement and design decisions. Object-oriented systems can directly implement the separation of *essence* and *accidents of implementation.*

There is great diversity in the implementation of the object-oriented ontology by way of programming language. Some languages render one or more of the elements of the object-oriented ontology in strict discipline, while others "adapt" the elements to their style or compatibility interests. Here are a few characteristic examples. Some languages (called "object-based") provide classes from which objects may be instantiated, but do not allow the definition of new classes. Some languages permit a child class to have multiple parent classes (multiple-inheritance), while others only permit (a less-confusing) single parent class inheritance relationship. Some languages enforce *encapsulation* strictly, while others allow direct access to data attributes without an intervening method activation. Some languages presume that message passing is synchronous rather than asynchronous. Some languages require services that may eventually be overridden to be prescribed as "override-able." In most cases, these "divergences" from the "pure" object-oriented paradigm can be "worked around," but to do so requires greater "mindset" discipline on the part of the modeler.

There may be many variations of language features that will influence the representation of the properties described in this chapter. Many new generations of object-oriented dialects will surely follow. Regardless, any language implementing the rubrics of the object-oriented ontology described here can facilitate a desirable balancing of the 15 *choice* properties pursuing a *thriving system*.

References

1. Waguespack LJ Jr, "'A Two-Page 'OO Green Card' for Students and Teachers," *Information Systems Education Journal*, 7 (61). http://isedj.org/7/61/. ISSN: 1545-679X, 2009 (A preliminary version appears in The Proceedings of ISECON 2007: §3743. ISSN: 1542-7382.)
2. Lakoff G. and Núñez R, *Where Mathematics Comes From: How the Embodied Mind Brings Mathematics into Being*, New York: Basic Books, 2000.
3. Alexander C, *The Nature of Order An Essay on the Art of Building and the Nature of the Universe: Book I - The Phenomenon of Life*, Berkeley, CA: The Center for Environmental Structure, 2002, p 238.
4. Coplien J and Schmidt D (Eds), *Pattern Languages of Program Design*, Reading, MA: Addison-Wesley, 1995.
5. Oxford American Dictionary, 2005.

Chapter 13
Promoting *Life* Using the Relational Paradigm

The concepts of system ecology and *life*-preserving transformations presented thus far can be integrated into any building process where *choices* are made. To further illustrate this integration and provide a contrast with that which is provided through the object-oriented paradigm, this chapter describes how these concepts can be realized in and are facilitated by the relational paradigm and engineering processes associated with it.

As with the object-oriented paradigm, a first step in this illustration is a survey of the defining characteristics of the relational paradigm independent of any of the programming languages used to represent or implement its features. The discussion begins with an ontology describing the paradigm's concepts and its vocabulary [1]. That is followed up by a review of each of the *life-preserving choice* properties and the opportunity that the relational paradigm provides for applying them.

13.1 An Ontology of the Relational Paradigm

This ontology is consistent with the practice in computer science and information science categorizing a domain of concepts (i.e. individuals, attributes, classes, and relationships). As before in our examination of the object-oriented paradigm, this ontology of the relational paradigm attempts to eschew the vestiges of implementation languages and development methodologies to expose the core nature and value of relational concepts based upon the work of E.F. Codd (Fig. 13.1) [2, 3].

The relational ontology is arranged as follows:

1. Individuals
2. Attributes
3. Classes
4. Relationships
   (a) Behavioral Relationships
      - Functional Dependency
      - Entity Integrity

L.J. Waguespack, *Thriving Systems Theory and Metaphor-Driven Modeling*,
DOI 10.1007/978-1-84996-302-2_13, © Springer-Verlag London Limited 2010

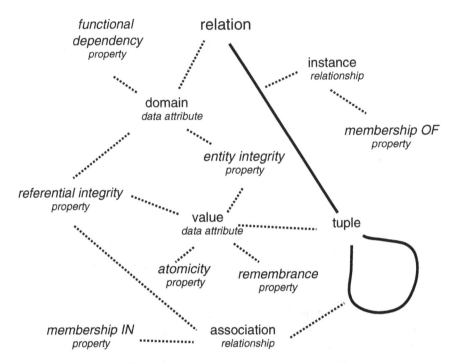

Fig. 13.1 The relational ontology

  (b) Association
- Relational Operations
- Join Compatibility
- Referential Integrity

  (c) Normalization
- First Normal Form
- Second Normal Form
- Third Normal Form

Individuals – The most concrete concept in the relational paradigm is the tuple.

Tuple – A tuple corresponds 1-1 with a single concept of reality that it represents. A tuple collects the facts that identify it as a single concept and the facts most closely identified with it.

Attributes – Attributes are those characteristics (facts) that describe a tuple. In the relational paradigm, attributes define data characteristics – each of which has a static and dynamic form. A prescribed set of attributes defines what is called the structure of a tuple. From inception to extinction, the structure of a tuple is immutable. The number of attributes in a tuple is called its degree.

Data Attributes – Data attributes store information (data) in the tuple and implement the property of remembrance. Remembrance is manifest in each attribute dynamically as "what is remembered," a particular data attribute value particular to each tuple derived from a data attribute domain that statically defines "what can be remembered," the possible values of the attribute.

Classes – The relational paradigm groups individuals into a collection called a relation. The relation corresponds directly to its mathematical antecedent where attribute values within each tuple reflect a correspondence with the coincidence of facts in the "real world," a correspondence (attribute relationship) that is shared by every tuple in that relation.

Relation – The relation concept combines both a definition of structure and the collection of tuple(s) based on that structure. A relation is defined as a fixed set of data attribute domains. Every tuple as an instance of a specific relation shares the same static structure defined by that relation with every other tuple of that relation. The relation concept thereby fuses the existence of the tuples to that of their relation; tuples cannot exist independent of their defining relation. Tuples are said to be members OF their relation. Tuples are added to or deleted from their relation. The order of attributes in a relation is insignificant except that the order is consistent for all tuples. A relation is also commonly called a table and each of its instances a row. The collection of data attribute value(s) for a particular data attribute from every row in a table is called a column.

Relationships – Relationships in the relational paradigm are based on the property of remembrance and the juxtaposition of data attribute values in one or more tuples in the same or across relations.

Behavioral Relationships – The behavioral relationships are all based upon the data attribute value(s) and which values are permitted to coexist in and across tuples and relations.

Functional Dependency – In a relation, a data attribute is functionally dependent when its data attribute value is always the same in any tuple for a given value in a second data attribute. In other words, the value of the first data attribute is determined by the value of the second; the second attribute is sometimes called the determinant. Functional dependency expresses the informational integrity of relations.

Entity Integrity – Entity integrity defines the twofold quality of tuple uniqueness in a relation: (a) every tuple in a relation is distinct in some data attribute value(s) from every other tuple in that relation or symmetrically, (b) there is a designated subset of data attributes (column(s)) called the primary key such that the data attribute value(s) of that data attribute(s) in that relation is distinct for all tuples and no values among them may be null (a value which is unknown and incomparable to any other value). There may be more than one subset of data attributes with the value characteristics of the primary key (each called a candidate key), but only one is designated as the primary key.

Association – An association is a relationship between tuples in the same or different relations. Tuples are intrinsically separable by way of entity integrity. At the same time, humans are compelled to categorize their experience of things in the physical world by superimposing groupings that collect tuples into sets. Tuples become members in a group based upon data attribute value(s). This property is called membership IN. This property also permits humans to identify a tuple that is not in a set (i.e. discrimination). (Membership IN an association is distinct from membership OF a relation, which is intrinsic by way of instance relationship.)

Relational Operations – Membership IN is realized through relational operations keying on relation structure and values. Each relational operation produces a real or virtual relation as its result. The selection operation retrieves tuple(s) based upon a selection predicate testing data attribute value(s) to determine whether each tuple is or is not in the set. Selection predicates are based on any boolean comparison including constant values or values referenced in data attribute value(s). The projection operation copies all the data attribute value(s) for a particular column(s). Association between relations (or a relation and itself) is based upon relating (matching) data attribute values in tuples of one relation with those of another. The join operation pairs every combination of tuples from one relation with those of another relation and copies the data attribute values from the pairs where the pairing satisfies a selection predicate. This relational operation is called join because facts from two sources are joined in the result.

Join Compatibility – Join compatibility requires that the values involved in comparisons (i.e. selection predicates) whether constants or data attribute values derive from the same data attribute domain.

Referential Integrity – When relations are devised such that a tuple in one relation predisposes the existence of (owns) tuple(s) in another, the data attribute(s) of the second required to join the relations is called a foreign key. Referential integrity asserts that any value found in the data value attribute(s) of a foreign key must appear in a tuple of the first relation as the value of a candidate key or itself be null.

Normalization – Relational model consistency depends on the semantic concurrence of the behavioral relationships and the objectives of the database modeler, the intension (rather than the accident of a relation's contents at any particular instant, its extension). The integrity properties defined above enable the database modeler to devise a structure and behavior of relations that avoid semantic discord called anomalies, the unintended loss or modification of information by relational operations. Relations designed to avoid certain kinds of anomalies are said to be normalized or in normal form. Normalization is the arrangement of data attributes and their relationships among relation structures to prevent particular anomalies.

First Normal Form – First Normal Form asserts that every data attribute value is atomic, indivisible in value or form, and may not be operated upon except as a whole and single value.

Second Normal Form – Second Normal Form is first normal form and asserts that every data attribute value not in the primary key is fully functionally dependent upon the primary key. ("Fully" means applying to every data attribute of the primary key.)

Third Normal Form – Third Normal Form presupposes first and second normal forms and asserts that no data attribute outside the primary key is transitively dependent upon the primary key. ("Transitively" means an attribute(s) functionally dependent upon an attribute functionally dependent upon an attribute (. . .) functionally dependent on the primary key.)

13.2 Modeling Living Structure in the Relational Paradigm

Chapter 2 recounted Christopher Alexander's theories of *wholeness* and *centers* explaining that the degree of *wholeness* derives from the strength or intensity that each *center* contributes to the whole. The strength or intensity of a *center* results from the intensity of the various 15 properties that he attributes to the *centers*. Recall that *centers* were recast as *choices* to map Alexander's theories of physical architecture onto the domain of information systems, their models, and architecture. Table 13.1 reproduces Table 3.1 for the reader's convenience and summarizes the 15 properties and their interrelationships along with their corresponding *choice* properties [4].

The discussion that follows examines each of the *choice* properties in turn and how each property relates to and may be facilitated by the relational paradigm. As these items derive from Alexander's property list, which was parsed from an experience of physical architecture, it is not surprising that the items in this list are often deeply interwoven in the promotion of *life* in the more abstract world of information systems.

Table 13.1 Properties of *Centers* mapped to *Choice* properties

	Alexander's Property	1	2	3	4	5	6	7	8	9	10	11	12	13	14	15	Choice property
1	Levels of Scale		*	*			*			*							Stepwise Refinement
2	Strong Centers			*			*		*	*			*		*		Cohesion
3	Boundaries		*		*			*	*	*	*						Encapsulation
4	Alternating Repetition		*			*	*		*	*					*		Extensibility
5	Positive Space	*	*	*			*	*		*		*		*			Modularization
6	Good Shape	*	*			*	*		*		*		*	*			Correctness
7	Local Symmetries	*			*					*				*			Transparency
8	Deep Interlock and Ambiguity				*	*				*			*	*		*	Composition of function
9	Contrast			*		*		*		*				*		*	Identity
10	Gradients	*	*				*		*			*	*			*	Scale
11	Roughness		*			*	*			*				*	*		User Friendliness
12	Echoes	*					*	*		*	*					*	Patterns
13	The Void	*		*	*		*		*						*		Programmability
14	Simplicity and Inner Calm					*	*					*	*			*	Reliability
15	Not Separateness			*		*			*		*	*		*	*		Elegance

13.2.1   Stepwise Refinement

Stepwise Refinement reliant upon Cohesion, Encapsulation, Correctness, and Identity (derived from Levels of Scale reliant upon Strong Centers, Boundaries, Good Shape, and Contrast) incorporated in the choice by the modeling action "to elaborate:"

In the *relational* paradigm, the strength of the information that a *relation* represents derives from the choice of *attributes* and their interdependence that form that entity of knowledge. Each *relation* depicts a cohesive, encapsulated, and distinct segment of knowledge. Each instance of that knowledge depends on its distinguishable *identity*: tuple by tuple. The scope of knowledge included in any particular model is constructed by the aggregation of these distinct segments interwoven through their explicit relationships. A whole model is built up stepwise as the "subset of the universe" chosen for the model (its *intension*) is systematically surveyed, cataloged, and defined in the collection of *relations*. Each *relation*'s integrity is achieved through its independent *correctness* separate and distinct except for those relations with which it maintains foreign key relationships. But the *correctness* of the whole proceeds from the assembly of the entire set of *relations* that together describe the reach of a model's responsibilities.

13.2.2   Cohesion

Cohesion reliant upon Extensibility, Transparency, Identity, Scale, Programmability, and Elegance (derived from Strong Centers reliant upon Alternating Repetition, Local Symmetries, Contrast, Gradients, The Void, and Not Separateness) incorporated in the choice by the modeling action "to factor:"

Each *relation* serves a separate, *cohesive* role in the responsibility of representing domain knowledge. *Relations* reflect *identity* as they distinctly capture and represent concepts in the form of facts collected to represent cogent, clearly defined information. The *tuples* within *relations* similarly represent cogent, unambiguously defined instances of reality patterned after the *attribute* structure of their containing *relation* while by virtue of their *entity integrity* they remain distinct from any other *tuple* therein. The population of *tuples* in a *relation* over time reflect the ebb and flow of experience that the *relation* captures in the dynamics of the represented reality (the *extension*). The *attribute* structure of the *relation* as a template for each of its *tuples* ensures that the experience remains comparable and thus understandable regardless of the number of instances that experience produces. *Functional dependency* and its role in *normalization* assure that each relation represents an unambiguous and atomic division of knowledge in the modeling space. The result is a collection of distinct knowledge experiences bound together by a structure that both explains the significance of each instance and enables the analysis of that experience in terms of the whole reality that the *relation* captures.

13.2.3   Encapsulation

> Encapsulation reliant upon Cohesion, Extensibility, Transparency, Composition of Function, Identity, and Scale (derived from Boundaries reliant upon Strong Centers, Alternating Repetition, Local Symmetries, Deep Interlock and Ambiguity, Contrast, and Gradients) incorporated in the choice by the modeling action "to encapsulate:"

In the *relational* paradigm, the individual *relation* assumes the responsibility for capturing and defining the "reality," the "facts" the modeler chooses to instill in a model. The modeler's *intension* is represented in the structure of facts that each of its instances must be able to remember. Each instance of the *relation* remembers by way of the *data attribute value* set in each *tuple*. The truthfulness of individual *tuples* can thus be independently established. An important part of the reality captured in each *tuple* is its individuality and the uniqueness of the information that it remembers in its *data attribute values*, its entity integrity. This individuality is determined solely by the values *encapsulated* therein dependent on no other information or relationships, as characterized by *Second Normal Form*.

13.2.4   Extensibility

> Extensibility reliant upon Cohesion, Modularization, Correctness, Composition of Function, Identity, and Elegance (derived from Alternating Repetition reliant upon Strong Centers, Positive Space, Good Shape, Deep Interlock and Ambiguity, Contrast, and Not Separateness) incorporated in the choice by the modeling action "to render extendable:"

Although each *relation* (down to the individual *tuple*) represents an independent depiction of reality in a relational model, more complex information is possible through the relationships that associate *relations*. *Associations* permit the depiction of more elaborate descriptions of a model's responsibilities. *Associations* depict correspondence, interdependence, or even ownership of concepts between and among *relations*. These *associations* are employed through the *relational operators* that combine or collect facts resident in multiple *relations* and render them correlated, organized, and/or extracted as a consistent but new representation of knowledge contained in the model.

13.2.5   Modularization

> Modularization reliant upon Stepwise Refinement, Cohesion, Encapsulation, Correctness, Transparency, Identity, User Friendliness and Programmability (derived from Positive Space reliant upon Levels of Scale, Strong Centers, Boundaries, Good Shape, Local Symmetries, Contrast, Roughness and The Void) incorporated in the choice by the modeling action "to modularize:"

By the nature of depicting model knowledge in a collection of individual *relations*, that knowledge is subdivided and compartmentalized. Furthermore, the process of *normalization* assures that the *intension* depicted by individual *relations* and combinations of *relations* through their *associations* is not ambiguous, redundant, or inconsistent. The compartmentalization of knowledge not only affords stakeholders a clearer view of relations individually, but also exposes the opportunities to safely recombine that knowledge through relational operations. This *cohesion* that distinguishes each relation's role in the *intension* of the model also segregates the concerns that accomplish the model's responsibilities and permits attention to be focused on relevant subsets of the overall model's complexity.

13.2.6   Correctness

Correctness reliant upon Stepwise Refinement, Cohesion, Modularization, Correctness, Composition of Function, Scale, Patterns, and Reliability (derived from Good Shape reliant upon Levels of Scale, Strong Centers, Positive Space, Good Shape, Deep Interlock and Ambiguity, Gradients, Echoes, and Simplicity and Inner Calm) incorporated in the choice by the modeling action "to align:"

Entity integrity, *referential integrity*, and *normalization* directly support a relational model's fidelity to the modeler's *intension*. *Entity integrity* assures that the uniqueness of each depiction of reality (*extension*) is enforced by the structure of the relation, *intension* (the *attribute* set, their respective *data attribute domains*, and the respective *functional dependencies*). The specification of that subset of *attributes* that will always contain a unique (combination of) value(s) defines the discriminating characteristics of that knowledge (the *primary key*) – the conformance to which is easily tested and thus protected. *Referential integrity* assures not only that *data attribute values* conform to the *intension* of their *relation's data attribute domain*, but further, to the modeled *intension* of *associations* between *tuples* including the ownership relationship between *relations*. *Normalization* extends the assurance of fidelity (model to the modeler's *intension*) by assuring that the interrelationship among *data attribute values* not only supports *entity integrity* and *referential integrity*, but also inhibits the accidental loss of model knowledge (*anomalies*) through the action of *relational operators*.

13.2.7   Transparency

Transparency reliant upon Stepwise Refinement, Modularization, Identity, and Programmability (derived from Local Symmetries reliant upon Levels of Scale, Positive Space, Contrast, and The Void) incorporated in the choice by the modeling action "to expose:"

The relational paradigm facilitates *transparency* in two obvious respects. Inspecting the relevant *data attribute values* is sufficient to assess every aspect of integrity whether *entity integrity* or *referential integrity*. These same continuously accessible values form the basis of all relationships among *data attribute values* or among *relations*. The consistency of each and every *data attribute value* can be certified. At any time before or after any and every relational database operation, we can verify concurrence with the time-independent definition of *intension* given by the *data attribute* set and their respective *data attribute domains* along with the designation of *candidate* and *foreign keys*. There are no implied or hidden definitions of *association* or dependence. Every aspect of *tuple* or *relation* fidelity is discerned through self-evident information. The result of any *relational operator* is determined solely by the *data attribute values* of the *relations* involved.

13.2.8 Composition of Function

Composition of Function reliant upon Extensibility, Modularization, Identity, User Friendliness, Patterns, and Programmability (derived from Deep Interlock and Ambiguity reliant upon Alternating Repetition, Positive Space, Contrast, Roughness, Echoes, and The Void) incorporated in the choice by the modeling action "to assemble:"

Each *relation* in a relational model represents a fundamental aspect of *intension* in the modeler's depiction of reality. *Association* and the use of *relational operators* effect that fundamental *intension* deriving an answer to any query we may invent based on that fundamental knowledge. The result of every *relational operation* is itself a *relation*. The modeler's ingenuity and discipline in forming queries carefully that yield results, *relations*, that are themselves consistent with the integrity constraints of the model creates the potential of an endless cascade of query result as input to another query and so on. This is the direct result of the mathematical formalism upon which the relation model is based – the predominating strength of the relational paradigm. The form in which these queries may be posed to a relational system is constrained only by the choice of mathematical representations (e.g. tuple calculus or domain calculus) or transformations (e.g. relational algebra or relational calculus) to the underlying relational definition.

13.2.9 Identity

Identity reliant upon Encapsulation, Modularization, Composition of Function, Scale, Programmability, and Elegance (derived from Contrast reliant upon Boundaries, Positive Space, Deep Interlock and Ambiguity, Gradients, The Void, and Not Separateness) incorporated in the choice by the modeling action "to identify:"

Identity is at the root of recognition. In the physical world, *identity* is literal based upon direct sensorimotor experience: by sight or touch and in some cases by sound or smell – a human experience of the "real" world. In the relational paradigm, this human experience is applied directly by collecting those *attributes* that completely describe how any particular instance is unique – the combination of *attributes* that comprise the *primary key*. The *primary key* serves to anchor the knowledge that surrounds it – those additional *attributes* that further describe the *tuple*, which it uniquely *determines* – those *attribute values* that are *functionally dependent* upon the *primary key*. No *tuple* is permitted to exist in the relational universe (*extension*) unless it has a *primary key* – *entity integrity*. Ownership as it is manifest through *foreign key associations* is anchored on the *primary key* of the owner *tuple*.

13.2.10 Scale

Scale reliant upon Stepwise Refinement, Cohesion, Transparency, Identity, User Friendliness, Patterns, and Elegance (derived from Gradients reliant upon Levels of Scale, Strong Centers, Local Symmetries, Contrast, Roughness, Echoes, and Not Separateness) incorporated in the choice by the modeling action "to focus:"

In many cases, the only familiarity that is needed in a relational model is the *intension* – the collection of *relation* definitions with their *attribute* sets defining their respective *attribute domains* and the *associations* among the *relations*. The *relational operators* are capable of extracting any and all knowledge from the *extension* of the tables because the *intension* defines the full potential of stored information based upon the semantic relationships. In terms of *scale*, any relational model (*intension* or *extension*) may be expanded to incorporate additional knowledge. The modeler achieves this by grafting new knowledge onto the existing *relation* structure through the addition and/or alignment of *data attribute domains* and *associations*.

13.2.11 User Friendliness

User Friendliness reliant upon Cohesion, Modularization, Correctness, Scale, Reliability, and Elegance (derived from Roughness reliant upon Strong Centers, Positive Space, Good Shape, Gradients, Simplicity and Inner Calm, and Not Separateness) incorporated in the choice by the modeling action "to accommodate:"

There is *elegance* in the succinctness and simplicity that arises from properly isolating domain knowledge in the respective *relations*. The use of user/client/customer familiar naming of *relations* and *attributes* and the choice of the commonly used, domain-based *attribute values* lends a comfort level to the representation of problem domain experience. The relational model also enables the derivation of contained knowledge at levels of granularity much higher than the individual *tuple* or *relation*. This is because *relational operations* on *relations* produce *relations* as their result. Information derived from a relational database can be presented as if it were simply retrieved from a single physical *relation*. This illusion is easily achieved in relational programming languages that support the definition and storage of queries that may then be referenced themselves as *relations* without the users' notice (i.e. *in ANSI SQL the "create view" syntax*). The facility of such extensions to apply relational operations so discretely creates virtually unlimited opportunities and permits what might otherwise be a complex and daunting algorithm of derivation to be completely ignored by the users.

13.2.12   Patterns

Patterns reliant upon Stepwise Refinement, Correctness, Transparency, Scale, User Friendliness, and Elegance (derived from Echoes reliant upon Levels of Scale, Good Shape, Local Symmetries, Gradients, Roughness, and Not Separateness) incorporated in the choice by the modeling action "to pattern:"

The most predominant *pattern* found in relational models is the regularity of structure that is embodied in the *tuples* that populate *relations*. This regularity assures that the same "questions" may be posed to each and every instance in a *relation* to elicit a consistently meaningful result. The *tuples* may be readily compared with one another and ordered that their factual content may be exhibited in a useful exposure of multiplicity. At the next level of structure, we find the *foreign key* relationship where an *association* between *relations* is constructed by choosing *attributes* in the two *relations* that proceed from the same *attribute domain*. The *pattern* is further emphasized by the property of *referential integrity*. This *pattern* of connecting facts between and among *relations* permits the stepwise assemblage of higher and higher levels of derived information. The *association* enables the traversal of a network of concepts and facts that are both defined by and operationally enabled by the *foreign key* construct. The use of these *patterns* by the relational model designer provides the opportunity to lay out domain knowledge in a predictable and usable mapping.

13.2.13   Programmability

Programmability reliant upon Stepwise Refinement, Encapsulation, Modularization, Transparency, Identity, and Reliability (derived from The Void reliant upon Levels of Scale, Boundaries, Positive Space, Local Symmetries, Contrast, and Simplicity and Inner Calm) incorporated in the choice by the modeling action "to generalize:"

Returning again to the use of *relational operations* to compose higher and higher levels of information, we see individual *relations* as building blocks that may be arranged (assembled through *relational operations*) to yield any reasonable arrangement or derivation of information that the underlying *relations* may possess. This is possible because of the individual *identity* that each *relation* fosters in its *tuples* and because of the predictable *reliability* that proceeds from the consistency and safety of *relational operations* that is guaranteed in a set of *normalized relations*. The extent of information mining that may be attempted is limited almost solely by the programmers' imagination.

13.2.14 Reliability

> Reliability reliant upon Correctness, Transparency, Patterns, Programmability, and Elegance (derived from Simplicity and Inner Calm reliant upon Good Shape, Local Symmetries, Echoes, The Void, and Not Separateness) incorporated in the choice by the modeling action "to normalize:"

There is an overarching simplicity that results from the fact that all of the properties of integrity are based upon *data attribute values* that may be readily inspected before or after any *relational operation. Intension* is expressed in modeled expressions of integrity constraints that are domain-specific. The synchronization between the *intension* and *extension* of the model is easily tested because of this simple *transparency. Reliability* is assured if valid *relational operations* are applied consistent with model integrity constraints and thus will always yield consistent ("truthful") information.

13.2.15 Elegance

> Elegance reliant upon Encapsulation, Modularization, Composition of Function, Scale, User Friendliness, Programmability, and Reliability (derived from Not Separateness reliant upon Boundaries, Positive Space, Deep Interlock and Ambiguity, Gradients, Roughness, The Void, and Simplicity and Inner Calm) incorporated in the choice by the modeling action "to coordinate:"

Elegance is achieved largely through the relational model when *relations* are modeled with a minimum of extraneous or redundant information. Indeed, eliminating redundancy is a common mantra of relational modeling. The laying out of basic facts divided into distinct *encapsulated* containers of knowledge and the subsequent composition of higher levels of derived information effects a sense of economy of form and abundant opportunity for exploring and extracting the knowledge that a database so fashioned accommodates.

13.3 Programming Languages Versus Ontology

The relational ontology may be applied supporting the 15 properties of *choice* derived from Christopher Alexander's theory of *wholeness* and *life*. However, only the integrity properties and *normalization* hint at the range of transactions that a relational model is usually composed to support. The absence of this explicit behavioral information restricts the modeler's ability to expose the elements of system development distinguished by Fred Brooks' as *essence* and *accidents of implementation*. The focus on data in the relational model to the effective exclusion of behavior results in models that predominate in their depiction of *essence* from the problem domain, but an *essence* that is almost entirely static in nature. The designation of *primary* and *foreign keys* and the process of *normalization* that imprints semantics on the static data structures only hints at the eventual range of behavior that will ensue in the operational descendent of the model, the physical relational database. A significant aspect of functional integrity depends almost exclusively on the highly disciplined application of relational operators over and above the relational paradigm's expressive power.

There are many language variations implementing features of the relational paradigm. More will come. Language implementations that support the rubrics of the relational ontology described here can contribute to achieving strength in the 15 properties of the *choices* expressing the data-centric essence of the stakeholder's intentions. The behavioral aspects of those intentions will require significant developer discipline.

References

1. Waguespack LJ, "The Relational Model Distilled to Support Data Modeling in IS 2002," *Information Systems Education Journal*, 8 (3). (2010), http://isedj.org/8/3/. ISSN: 1545-679X. (A preliminary version appears in The Proceedings of ISECON 2009: §3133. ISSN: 1542-7382.)
2. Codd, EF, "Derivability, Redundancy and Consistency of Relations Stored in Large Data Banks", IBM Research Report, 1969.
3. Codd, EF, "A Relational Model of Data for Large Shared Data Banks", Communications of the ACM, 13, 6 (June 1970): 377–387.
4. Alexander C, *The Nature of Order An Essay on the Art of Building and the Nature of the Universe: Book I - The Phenomenon of Life*, Berkeley, CA: The Center for Environmental Structure, 2002, p. 238.

Chapter 14
Thriving Systems Through Metaphor-Driven Modeling

Computer-based information systems are certainly among the most complex constructions conceived by humankind. And more often than not, those constructions that may be more complex include embedded information systems of some kind. To address the total range of issues and all the variations of process that are or can be employed in the development of information systems is far beyond the scope of this monograph. Thus, the goal here is to focus on the modes of perception, representation, and understanding that lead to the success of all those efforts expended regardless of any particular paradigm, technology, or methodology – and in doing so, to propose an enlightened context within which to consider those paradigms, technologies, and methodologies. Alexander's conception of system *life*, Lakoff et al.'s depiction of human understanding and cognition, and Brooks' insights for discerning the *essential* difficulties in building information systems converge to form that enlightened context.

14.1   No Perfect Models: Only Useful Ones

Hopefully, this discussion on information systems, architecture, and models crystallizes the proposition that for any given system in the natural world, science and engineering cannot construct a perfect model. This is so for at least the following reasons:

1. *If perfect model means "truthful to the given purpose," then perfection fails because "truth" depends on human perception, and given the divergent perceptions of a stakeholder community, there are at best several "truths" – if any one suffices as "truth."*
2. *The fundamental purpose of a model is to "escape the truth" by omitting and/or substituting for system characteristics to yield a representation that can be manipulated to serve the intentions of the stakeholders and (particularly among them) developers.*

L.J. Waguespack, *Thriving Systems Theory and Metaphor-Driven Modeling*,
DOI 10.1007/978-1-84996-302-2_14, © Springer-Verlag London Limited 2010

3. *Discounting the above-mentioned reasons, even if a "perfect" model could be generated, it would only be "perfect" for that instant of the "now," the "present," because the dynamic nature of all living systems, in an ever-changing context, means that all models are instantly "out of sync" with the reality they purport to depict.*

Although there may be no perfect models, there are, however, *useful models*. Useful models answer specific, predetermined questions, and permit developers (and other stakeholders) to achieve particular goals. Models are "truthful" and are useful when:

1. *Both the stakeholder goals and the specific, predetermined questions are explicit.*
2. *The features of the model accord with these goals and questions.*
3. *The model features permit stakeholders a means of assessing their individual and corporate satisfaction.*

A wide variety of models at various levels of detail and with various stakeholder perspectives is possible. In every case, creating or engineering these as useful models proceeds from the same fundamentals: Christopher Alexander's theory that structures that exhibit *life* possess a quality that resonates with their observers' sense of order. This resonance makes a structure at the same time understandable, effective, and satisfying. Those basic facets of order that observers recognize in physical architecture are characterized in the 15 properties of *centers,* as Alexander defines them. In systems (information systems), those facets of order are recognizable in the 15 *choice* properties.

14.2 Processes That Generate Useful Models

The pace of change in information systems is markedly faster than in physical architectural structures. Useful information system models require an even greater emphasis on accommodating change than physical structures. In most cases, experience with information systems is more conceptual than physical for the stakeholders. That makes the stakeholders' intentions more illusive and more ephemeral, and in need of constant remodeling. These complexities underscore the importance of responsiveness to change in any approach to generating useful models. In this regard, Alexander's theory of order benefits greatly from Brook's "*essence and accident*" and Lakoff's "*understanding through metaphor.*"

Three fundamental concepts must permeate the systems engineering mindset to achieve useful models.

1. *A model (e.g. an information system) as an enculturated[1] organism is grown and must be nurtured as such. It thrives only when its unfolding preserves a structure that exhibits life* [1].

---

[1]Enculturation: "the process by which an individual learns the traditional content of a culture and assimilates its practices and values," Merriam-Webster Online. 19 February 2010.

2. *A model is only perceived as successful if it faithfully reflects the essence of its purpose as understood by the community of its stakeholders* [2].
3. *A model is a conceptual metaphor in an ever-changing reality, a humanly perceived reality* [3, 4].

14.3 Useful Models as Enculturated Organisms

Alexander's theory of living structure provides 15 properties contributing to *life*, which when mapped to the properties of *choices* apply at every level of modeling in system development. They are not only relevant, but developers *must* pursue them at every level if the *essence* that defines the combined (integrated) intention of the stakeholders is to survive the model *unfolding* process. The *essence* perceived by each stakeholder must be preserved and reflected with satisfying clarity. Herein lies the value of the metaphor-driven aspect of the process. Models as metaphors can capture all the stakeholder-perceived *essence(s)*, while including whatever additional accidents are needed to package them coherently. As a package, it may be broader, more comprehensive, and/or less simplistic than any particular stakeholder may expect, but *their essence* is there. Therein lies the challenge of effective representation, capturing the *essence*, despite the preconceptions of appearance that the stakeholders may hold otherwise. The challenge is to distill the *essence* from the camouflage of the *accidents of implementation* with which the stakeholders may identify it (symptoms rather than causes, side effects rather than business rules). In a sense, this requires the modeler and stakeholders to seek a deeper meaning than their casual perception of the *essence* – a meaning *not separated from* the whole but in concert with it, *elegantly*.

Not every modeling project is destined for computer-based implementation. The goal may be documentation, explanation, or formal analysis of a system and/or its processes. In any event, the 15 properties still apply at the level of detail and with the focus on issues deemed most relevant (or troublesome) at that level of perception. In information systems modeling for business applications, there are three commonly recognized levels of perception at which modeling is aimed. These levels reflect the preoccupation of the particular community of stakeholders sponsoring the modeling task, or may represent perceived plateaus of abstraction exposing *choices* that must be determined at that level. The following graphic (see Fig. 14.1) represents a typical three-tiered stratification of modeling focus from the general vision of the business to the detailed definition of its supporting information system(s).

Each of these modeling layers (business model, business process model, and software model) draws its feature sensitivity from the concerns for control and survivability (*life*) experienced most often by modelers at that level. Culture, history, tradition, and custom (among others) have shaped a perspective, vocabulary, and presumptions about each layer.

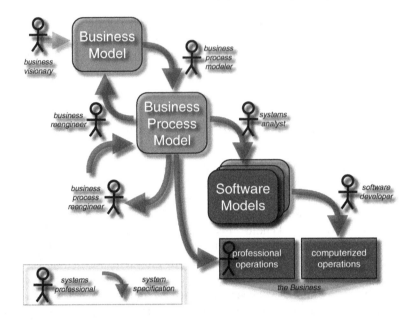

Fig. 14.1 Typical system modeling layers

14.4   Modeling the Business Organism

The business model level focuses on those elements that inform the business goals and strategy. It attempts to include all the elements that either need to be "managed" or influence the "management decisions." The following graphic (Fig. 14.2) and corresponding list represent concerns attributed to the business model level [5].

- *Value propositions: The company's offerings that bundle products and/or services into value for the customer. A value proposition creates utility for the customer.*
- *Target customer segments: The customer segments that a company wants to offer value to. This describes the groups of people with common characteristics for which the company creates value. The process of defining customer segments is referred to as market segmentation.*
- *Distribution channels: The various means of the company to get in touch with its customers. This describes how a company goes to market. It refers to the company's marketing and distribution strategy.*
- *Customer relationships: The links that a company establishes between itself and its different customer segments. The process of managing customer relationships is referred to as customer relationship management.*
- *Value configurations: The configuration of activities and resources.*
- *Core capabilities: The capabilities and competencies necessary to execute the company's business model.*

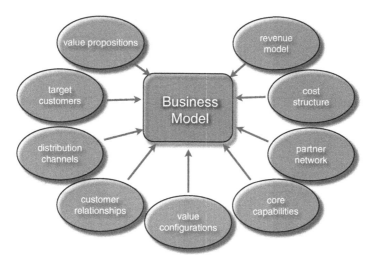

Fig. 14.2 Typical business model attributes

- *Partner network*: *The network of cooperative agreements with other companies necessary to efficiently offer and commercialize value. This describes the company's range of business alliances.*
- *Cost structure*: *The monetary consequences of the means employed in the business model.*
- *Revenue model*: *The way a company makes money through a variety of revenue flows.*

14.5 Modeling the Business Process Organism

The business process model level represents management's translation of the business goals and strategy into organizational structure and operations. It attempts to include all the elements that either need to be "managed" or influence the "management decisions" concerning the effectiveness and efficiency of executing the business plan. The following graphic (Fig. 14.3) and corresponding list represent typical concerns attributed to the business process model level [6].

- *Resources*: *Abstract (i.e. information, intellectual property) and physical (i.e. people, facilities, machinery) involved in the execution of business practice to achieve a business objective.*
- *Processes*: *Business activities defined by a purpose, steps, and a goal – described by process owner, the actors in the process, the priority in the business, timing constraints, cost, and potential outcomes.*
- *Goals*: *The purpose of the business process, characterized by both quantitative (how many, how much) and qualitative (how well, how good), suitable for measurement and assessment.*

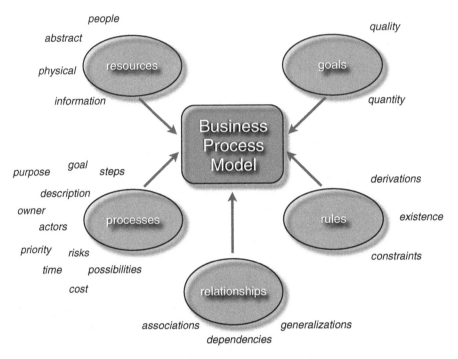

Fig. 14.3 Typical business process model attributes

- *Rules*: *The controls on the business function including how knowledge/resources may be transformed, limitations on process behavior, or resource consumption and characterization of business stability.*
- *Relationships*: *The interdependency in time and resource of various business processes including generalization/specialization and association/aggregation.*

14.6   Modeling the Software Organism

The information systems level of modeling depicts the focus on information system specific static and dynamic structures leading to programming and implementation (e.g. file formats, communication protocols, programming language syntax and development tools, operating system features, data management services, networking, and storage structures). The following graphic (Fig. 14.4) depicts the modeling components typically documented using the Unified Modeling Language, UML [7].

As diverse, as complex, or as specialized may be any of the issues of concern at any level, they all constitute *choices*. Every stakeholder's satisfaction with each *choice* is affected by the 15 *choice* properties contributing to their perception of *life* in one way or another. It seems quite unlikely that all the properties can be

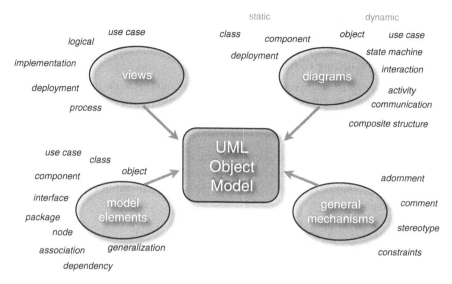

Fig. 14.4 Modeling elements represented by UML

measured or applied at every *choice*. However, a modeler with the *life*-preserving mindset based on the 15 properties is equipped to take advantage of opportunities to guide each model's *unfolding,* while preserving its *life*.

14.7 Disambiguating Essence and Accident

The *essence* that is relevant at each modeling level is the same, but the aspect from which the stakeholders may view it will be quite different. To move from a vision of a business to a business model requires making *choices* that arise because of environment: geography, climate, or culture. These *choices* incorporate *accidents of implementing* the business vision. It is important at this level to identify these issues as *accidents,* lest they are misinterpreted as *essence*, elements of architecture, which needlessly misdirect the *unfolding* that will follow. Each level introduces its own *accidents of implementation*. The recognition and declaration of the distinction between *essence* and *accident* are critical to the *unfolding* of the model and perhaps, even more importantly, to what is usually called maintenance, and often results in the majority of the cost of ownership. (Maintenance is usually a misnomer, as rather than repairing an error of some sort, the activity is actually redefining some aspect of a model's functionality. In this sense, it is actually the next stage of development – the next stage of *unfolding*.)

It is well noted that missteps in the development of a system are far more costly to remediate the longer they persist in a system. One example of that is the erroneous acceptance of a *choice* as essential when it is not – as when the answer "That's the way we've always done it!" ends the requirements' discovery and analysis process prematurely rather than triggering a test to distinguish *essentiality* from "habitual-ity."

Admitting to the significance of *essence* and *accident* leads to a somewhat surprising, but crystallizing realization:

> **Analysis** is all about identifying and separating **essence** from **accidents** in the process of understanding and then modeling those system characteristics.

> **Design** is about preserving the **essence** while choosing and encapsulating the **accidents** as models progress from understanding toward deploying an implementation.

Systems analysis and design together form one *life*-preserving process in modeling and building. The process succeeds as the product comes together with the evolving, *unfolding* requirements, effectively reconciling the intentions of the community of stakeholders.

14.8   Models Unfolding as Metaphors

The intentions of the community of stakeholders form an ever-moving target reflecting the stakeholder community and the world they inhabit. As Lakoff's results have shown, it is plausible to say that (as well as they can be) all the stakeholders' own intentions are formed as metaphors intimating the reality they desire to achieve. These metaphors and their intentions are sometimes indistinct and evolving – "as through a glass, darkly."[2] Hence, not only the system environment, but also the stakeholders' own understanding of the system is an ever-moving target. This realization has led to development methodologies that emphasize the feedback loop between design and analysis, where partially constructed models become transfigured renditions of the stakeholders' expressed intentions and can be "held up to the light" permitting stakeholders to confirm or deny for themselves if their "metaphors" express their intentions for the system and lead to satisfying model results.

14.9   The Pace of Life

Pursuing a convergence of model features with stakeholder intentions is a perpetual process, lasting as long as the system exists, as long as the stakeholder community agrees that they require it, and as long as it has *life*. If the intentions evolve rather slowly, then there may be a sense of stability requiring modest and infrequent attention. If, on the other hand, the intentions and the environment are volatile, there will

---

[2] 1 Corinthians 13, New Testament.

be a sense of endless flux demanding continuous *unfolding,* chasing faithfulness to the stakeholder intentions. In either case, the Modeling Checklist for the Living Information System is a guide to that pursuit of faithfulness.[3]

14.10   Engineering Thriving Systems

Systems engineering should focus on the *essence,* while software engineering focuses on the *accidents.* Software engineering provides resources (tools and methodologies) for crafting *accidents of implementation,* which exhibit dexterity and agility – the ability to respond quickly and economically to a changing environment and the arrival of new and more effective technology options. In either case, success depends on incorporating the same underlying fundamentals – the *essence* and *accidents* must be identified, segregated, and encapsulated so that the *unfolding* process of the system's models preserves the *essence* and strengthens *life* rather than endangering it. The quality of *life* is assessable through the strength of the 15 properties of *choices.* Only if *life* is preserved and strengthened in the ongoing *unfolding* of the system's models is it possible to achieve and sustain the beauty of a *thriving system* we may seek.

References

1. Alexander C, *The Nature of Order An Essay on the Art of Building and the Nature of the Universe: Book I - The Phenomenon of Life,* The Center for Environmental Structure, Berkeley, CA, 2002.
2. Brooks FP, "No Silver Bullet: Essence and Accidents of Software Engineering," *Computer,* Vol. 20, No. 4 (April 1987) pp 10–19.
3. Lakoff G and Johnson M, *Philosophy in the Flesh,* Basic Books, New York, 1999.
4. Lakoff G. and Johnson M, *Metaphors We Live By,* University of Chicago Press, Chicago, IL, 1980.
5. http://en.wikipedia.org/wiki/Business_model, accessed 1/25/2010.
6. Adapted from http://en.wikipedia.org/wiki/Business_process_model, accessed 1/25/2010.
7. Adapted from MDA Guide V1.0.1, http://www.omg.org/cgi-bin/doc?omg/03-06-01.pdf

[3]See Section 10.7.

Epilogue

From the outset of this monograph, I have attempted to be forthright with the reader:

The ideas and propositions that follow are not at the stage of provability but rather are postulation. The primary arguments associate and relate concepts that proceed from three very distinct intellectual perspectives. In this, the goal is to encourage builders of information systems to consider a new, innovative perspective with which to assess the value, the quality, of the constructions they envision and implement. I align well-respected findings and theories projecting the significance of one concept upon another by exposing what I believe are largely intuitive, self-evident correlations once the concepts are explained in the manner chosen here. The explanations draw predominantly from a practitioner's perspective encouraging the reader to be an active participant by recalling personal experience reframed by the perspectives offered here.[1]

I do not presume that the presentation here is totally transparent or even, perhaps, convincing. However, I am hopeful that this perspective on modeling (and design) and the insights of Alexander, Lakoff, and Brooks that I have attempted to weave together lead you to consider further whether there really is a "nature of order" that underlies our ability to know about and understand the systems we encounter or at least that we perceive. There is no denying that to ignore the "nature of order" found in "creation" (i.e. biology, geology, physics, ecology, etc.) results in varying degrees of disharmony and (not so infrequently) extinction.

To encounter a parallel between the "order" in nature and the satisfying qualities of human-made systems is at the same time surprising and comforting. It is surprising because nature is so often perceived as *life* wild and uncontrolled while the intention of human-made systems is *life* rendered organized and reliable. In this discussion of *living structures*, *unfolding*, and *metaphor* as perception of reality, it is comforting to consider that the success of constructing information systems for which we have only about a century's worth of experience may be informed by the natural world around us that has thus far succeeded in surviving countless millions of times longer. There must be something in the order of nature that can lead us in the direction toward organization and reliability far beyond humankind's record of success in devising systems thus far!

---

[1]See Section 1.5

Index